THE POCKET
GUIDE TO NESTS AND EGGS

Collins
Pocket Guide Books

NATURAL HISTORY

COLLINS POCKET GUIDE TO BRITISH BIRDS
by R. S. R. Fitter
Illustrated by R. A. Richardson

COLLINS POCKET GUIDE TO WILD FLOWERS
by R. S. R. Fitter and David McClintock
Illustrated by Seven Artists

COLLINS POCKET GUIDE TO THE SEA SHORE
by John Barrett and C. M. Yonge
Illustrated by Seven Artists

GENERAL

COLLINS POCKET GUIDE TO GOOD COOKING
by Robin McDouall
Illustrated

COLLINS POCKET GUIDE TO THE UNDERSEA WORLD
Written and Illustrated by Ley Kenyon

*

Other Books
by R. S. R. Fitter

THE ARK IN OUR MIDST

LONDON'S NATURAL HISTORY
(*in the New Naturalist Library*)

BIRDS OF TOWN AND VILLAGE
(*in the Country Naturalist Series*)

LONDON'S BIRDS

The
Pocket Guide to
NESTS AND EGGS

By
R. S. R. FITTER

assisted by
THE HON. GUY CHARTERIS

Illustrated by
R. A. RICHARDSON

COLLINS
ST JAMES'S PLACE, LONDON

First published 1954
Second Impression 1959
Third Impression 1961

PRINTED IN GREAT BRITAIN
COLLINS CLEAR-TYPE PRESS : LONDON AND GLASGOW

It is a fascinating pursuit, when there is leisure for it, to look for the nests in the garden or neighbourhood of a country home. The discovery of a well-hidden nest with eggs gives a sense of delicate privilege; the watching of its subsequent welfare is a continuing interest; and if the end is happy and the young birds leave the nest safely, we feel deeply satisfied. Yet birds, if they could address us might well say, 'However kindly your interest and however benevolent your intention, please do not look for our nests. You will expose them to dangers of which you do not dream and from which you cannot save them.'

VISCOUNT GREY OF FALLODON, *The Charm of Birds*

I can suck melancholy out of a song as a weasel sucks eggs.

JAQUES, *As You Like It*

Ever since I can remember sensation I have been delighted by the sight of birds' eggs. They represent for me a kind of beauty which to this day nothing supplants.

PAUL NASH, *Outline*

I began to hate myself for catching and killing summer butter-flies and for taking birds' eggs.

FRANK KENDON, *The Small Years*

HOW TO FIND
THE NEST YOU WANT

IF YOU WANT to look up a nest you already know, there is an index beginning on page 167.

If you want to identify an unfamiliar nest there are three main lines of approach:

DESCRIPTIVE SECTION, pages 16–134. All the birds you are likely to find nesting in Britain are arranged in order of SIZE, grouped under the main headings of *Land, Waterside* and *Water*. The section begins with the smallest British land bird, the goldcrest, and ends with our largest water bird, the mute swan. The size groupings are based on the relative sizes of such well-known birds as the sparrow and the pheasant.

THE ILLUSTRATIONS. 40 colour plates and 8 plates in black-and-white between text pages 112 and 113 provide you with the means of identifying a nest *visually*, for here the nests are grouped according to the sort of situation in which you are likely to find them, e.g. all the nests in holes in trees are together in one group of plates.

THE KEY, pages 135–153. This affords a special method of easy identification by enabling you to cross-check according to the information available. An example of how to use the Key is given on page 136. The Key is divided as follows:

Colonial and Social Nesting. On page 137 you can see if a bird has a habit of nesting close to other birds of the same species.

Nest Sites. Between pages 138 and 142 you can look up a nest under fifteen different site groupings.

vii

Nest Construction. On page 143 you can look up certain peculiarities of the construction of nests, such as domes or access by a short runway.

Nest Materials. On pages 144 and 145 you can check to see if your nest is made of any of the more unusual nest materials.

Egg Shape. On pages 146 and 147 you can look to see which birds have eggs shaped not like the familiar egg of the breakfast table, but round, elliptical or pear-shaped.

Egg Colour. Between pages 148 and 151 you can look up the eggs under their colouring, and whether or not they are spotted.

Nestlings. If your nest has not eggs but nestlings, you can look them up on pages 152 and 153, where they are classified according to the colour of the inside of the mouth.

ACKNOWLEDGMENTS

AS WITH *The Pocket Guide to British Birds,* I could never have written this book without the help of many kind friends, nor achieved it so expeditiously without being able to check my own notes, which extend over a period of thirty-one years, against the invaluable contributions of the Rev. F. C. R. Jourdain to *The Handbook of British Birds.* Time and again I have been driven back to his exact wording as the only accurate description of a nest or an egg. On some aspects of breeding biology his work has become almost definitive, though on others, as he would have been the first to acknowledge, there is still very much to be learnt. Bruce Campbell's *Finding Nests* was published soon after my first draft was completed, so that I was also able to consult his unrivalled knowledge of the siting and construction of nests when revising the book for the press.

Among those I should like to thank especially are my wife, for much attention to loose English and other tiresome details during the writing stage; Richard Richardson, both for reading the manuscript and for being patient over many finicking suggestions for improving the plates; Geoffrey Dent, James Fisher, Helen Rait Kerr and Alec Robertson, for wise advice during the planning and teething stage; R. P. Bagnall-Oakeley, Curator of the Montagu egg collection at Gresham's School, Holt, and E. A. Ellis, of the Castle Museum, Norwich, for putting their fine collections of eggs and skins at the artist's disposal; and, for help of kinds too various to specify, W. B. Alexander, W. Bishop, C. D. Borrer, P. Clarke, P. D. Kirby, R. M. Lockley, Mrs. R. F. Meiklejohn, D. Nethersole-Thompson and the Wildfowl Trust. The tiresome chore of compiling the index was most efficiently done by my wife with the help of our daughter Jenny, to both of whom I am most grateful.

Finally, anybody who knows Guy Charteris's encyclopaedic knowledge of the nesting habits of European birds will realise what an enormous help it has been to have him at my elbow at every stage of drafting, proof correction and scanning of the plates, and to be able to consult his fine collection of eggs. Without his aid it would have taken me much longer to complete the book. Earlier I said that often I had been driven back to Jourdain's descriptions; now I can add that usually it was Charteris who drove me. I can only hope that he feels this book to be not too inferior a shrine to contain some of the manifold knowledge of birds' eggs and nests which he has acquired in the course of a lifetime. For my part I rejoice to think that a book of mine has become the repository of much knowledge that perhaps might not otherwise have found a printed record.

Last of all, a personal detail. There still exists vividly in my mind's eye my first bird's nest, at the age of five, a blackbird's against a tree-trunk in a Middlesex hedgerow long since sub-merged under houses and gardens, and how bitterly I wept when the one egg taken from that nest for me got broken. I only hope that this book may help others to get pleasure out of observing the nests and eggs of birds, and that they will not weep bitterly because nobody will take an egg out of the nest for them.

R.S.R.F.

Chinnor, January 1954

CONTENTS

PLATES IN COLOUR

Nests are arranged broadly according to their sites. For general notes on the arrangement of the plates, see p. 15. All plates, both in Colour and in Black-and-White, are to be found between text pages 112 and 113.

*The colour and black-and-white reproductions were engraved by
Messrs. Odhams Photo-Engravers, London*

PLATES IN
BLACK-AND-WHITE

*The plates in Black-and-White follow after Colour plate No. 40.
All plates, both in Colour and in Black-and-White, are to be found
between text pages 112 and 113.*

Take the Book to the Nest

NOT

the Egg to the Book

INTRODUCTION

THIS BOOK is designed as a companion to *The Pocket Guide to British Birds*. It has two features to be found in no previous book on British birds' nests and eggs: there is an illustration of every British breeding bird at its nest, and it approaches the subject from the angle of identification in the field, and not from that of collecting and placing in a cabinet drawer. While I was writing *The Pocket Guide to British Birds*, which was intended to help the beginner in bird-watching to identify any bird he was reasonably likely to see in the British Isles, I was constantly aware of its deficiency in one important particular. It makes scarcely any mention of nests, eggs or any other part of the breeding cycle, although these may be important clues to the identity of a bird. Moreover, one often stumbles on a nest before being aware that the bird is present at all, and perhaps even more often one flushes a bird from its nest without getting a proper view of it.

The present book now seeks to fill the gap, and to supply the information that had to be omitted if the other book was to be kept down to pocket size—information, moreover, which is only needed during the spring and summer months. Its aim is to enable people to identify any nest with eggs or young that they may find in their garden, in the open country, or by the seaside, in the British Isles. As in *The Pocket Guide to British Birds* the accent throughout is on identification. There is no attempt, for instance, to explain *how* to find nests. This particular task has been done superbly by Dr. Bruce Campbell in *Finding Nests* (Collins, 12s 6d), a book that has become a standard work and indispensable to the field naturalist.

A special word of warning is necessary about covering up your tracks after you have found a nest. Many other animals and birds—stoats, weasels, rats, squirrels both red and grey, jays, crows, jackdaws, magpies, gulls, snakes—are constantly on the look-out for a meal of eggs or young birds. Many nests have to be approached through long grass or thick undergrowth, so that it is almost impossible not to leave a trail which one of these predators will be only too ready to follow. How often do you find, in visiting a nest a second time, that it has been robbed? You may feel inclined to blame the small boy next door, but it is just as likely to have been a weasel or a magpie. Therefore, anybody who finds a nest needs to take special care that no person, animal or bird coming afterwards can see where he has been. Put your own private mark if you like, so that you know how to find it again yourself, but don't bend back a twig that was shielding it from view, or break down the nettles, or hook back a briar.

There are comparatively few nests of British birds that can be identified at first glance by some conspicuous feature, such as the magpie's dome of sticks, the long-tailed tit's lichen-covered 'bottle', or the song-thrush's bare mud lining. Many eggs cannot be identified away from their nests even by experts, and the great majority are liable to baffle the beginner when seen only in the pocket handkerchief or the cabinet drawer. Nestlings are even worse, if anybody was so foolish as to try and identify them away from their nest. To identify the great majority of nests with any degree of certainty, habitat, site and materials must all be taken into account, together with the description of either eggs or young. Even then there are often nests to which the parents must be watched back and identified first before absolute certainty can be achieved. In such cases this book must be used in conjunction with *The Pocket Guide to British Birds*, for it does not repeat the information given there on how to identify the adult birds.

It cannot be emphasised too strongly that the bird and its nest and eggs or young are a unity. That is why the bird, the nest and the eggs are here illustrated together for every species that breeds in the British Isles, whether regularly or irregularly. Most previous books that have dealt in any detail with birds' nests and eggs have shown the eggs in serried ranks as if in a cabinet drawer. This inevitably fostered the idea of the egg as an isolated object in itself rather than only one link in the chain

2

of a bird's life. Admittedly many eggs are objects of beauty, but so are flowers, and both look even more beautiful in their natural surroundings than in the best designed artificial setting.

In the past, ornithology, like every other branch of natural history, had to go through a phase of collection, identification and classification, so that basic facts could be established and descriptions written. The collection of eggs, by both amateurs and professionals, was a necessary part of this important stage in the advance of ornithology to scientific status, and as in so many other branches of natural history the amateur often made as great a contribution as the professional, if not greater. Now, however, we have reached the end of that stage. The further advances to be expected from the continued indiscriminate collection of eggs do not justify any general licence to do so. At the same time I would wish neither to decry the valuable work done in the past by the Rev. F. C. R. Jourdain, E. C. Stuart Baker, John Walpole-Bond and others, nor to deny the possible need of the taking of eggs for approved scientific purposes in the future. But the making of private collections of eggs is one of those activities that no longer fit in with the climate of the times, like many other pursuits that flourished before 1914, but now languish. If as many people indulged in it as watch football, there would soon be no birds left to lay eggs. Today there is a growing army of bird-lovers who prefer to watch their birds right through the breeding cycle and naturally resent any attempt to interrupt that cycle at an early stage. Too much valuable time has been spent by bird-protectionists and egg-collectors in slanging each other, and chasing each other, and it is my earnest hope that both parties will before long be able to settle down to work together for the welfare of the birds, which both have ultimately at heart.

MAKING NOTES

THE PRESENT BOOK is designed to be carried in the pocket, so that the book can be taken to the nest, not the egg to the book, if identification is needed. If, however, you should stumble on a nest when you are without the book, never take an egg back with you. Except in the very early stages, before incubation has begun, it is no good putting it back again a few hours later, for it will never hatch once it has cooled. Moreover, even experts often fail to identify a single egg. And then when you have got the egg, the temptation to start a 'one only' collection may be strong. As to that, I need only quote the excuse of the nurse in *Midshipman Easy*: 'If you please, ma'am, it was a very little one'.

However, don't go to the other extreme and rely on your memory. No instrument is so fallible as the human memory, and it always passes my understanding what an absolute trust our courts of law seem to place on people's recollections of things that happened months ago. It is essential to make notes on the spot, and I suggest the following headings:

Habitat: e.g. kitchen garden.
Nest site: 5 ft. up in fruit tree against wall.
Eggs: four; blue-green with reddish brown spots.
Nest material: dried grass and roots, lined with dried grass.
(*Young:* sparse down, yellow mouth.)

This of course makes it a blackbird's.

If you see the parent bird, and do not know it, then follow the suggestions for note-taking in *The Pocket Guide to British Birds,* pp. 2–4.

BIRD RINGING

WHEREAS forty or fifty years ago those bird enthusiasts who specialised in the finding and identification of nests were egg collectors almost to a man, nowadays they are nearly all bird ringers. For the convenience of those who pursue this increasingly popular scientific 'sport', the appropriate ring size is given in the text for each regular breeding species.

Bird-ringing schemes began in Britain about forty-five years ago and on the Continent a few years earlier, and have led to many remarkable advances in our knowledge of how and where birds migrate, and of how long they live in the wild state. Thus we now have positive proof that our cuckoos and swallows go to Africa in the winter, that our fieldfares come to us from Scandinavia every autumn and return there in the spring to breed, and that the average expectation of further life for robins of all ages after their first few months is one year.

The process of ringing consists in affixing a small aluminium ring to the bird's leg and letting it go again. Every ring is individually numbered and bears the address of the British Museum (Natural History), London, S.W.7, from which the Bird Ringing Committee of the British Trust for Ornithology, which runs the British ringing scheme, operates. Since some risk to the bird is involved if it is handled inexpertly, only fairly experienced bird-watchers are permitted to take direct responsibility for ringing. Full details of the ringing scheme and how to get permission to take part in it may be had from the Secretary of the British Trust for Ornithology at 2 King Edward Street, Oxford.

Some brief hints on ringing nestlings may be of assistance to those who are able to take part in the ringing scheme, either directly or through a school or local natural history society. The rings are issued in eleven sizes (1, SO, 1A, 2, 3, Double-ended, 4, Clip 4, 16 mm., 19 mm., and M), and made up in packets of twenty.

5

It is a very good plan, on receipt of a supply of rings, to arrange them in numerical order on a string, wire or large safety-pin.

Most nestling song-birds can be ringed safely when about half-grown, by which time their legs have lost their early pliability and begun to assume the thickness of the adults' legs. On the other hand, it is dangerous to wait till they are almost fully fledged, for the nestlings of many species 'explode' and jump from the nest if disturbed a few days before they would normally leave. Even if they do not actually jump out, they may be difficult or impossible to put back again, especially if one of the brood utters the shrill alarm cry. It is a good plan to 'brood' over each nestling with the palm of the hand as it is returned to the nest, until you are quite sure it is settled in again. Needless to say, it is extremely dangerous for young birds to leave the nest before they are ready to fly, as they are especially vulnerable to cats, weasels and other predators, so that a heavy responsibility rests on the ringer who risks ringing a brood if they look at all near to their fledging time. Experience will teach that look of nervous expectancy which young birds acquire when they are soon to leave the safety of the nest, and the rather puddingy appearance of nestlings that are still some way off being fledged. As a very rough guide with young song-birds, if you know approximately the day the birds were hatched, you can divide their fledging period into four quarters, and assume that for the first two quarters they are too young to be ringed, for the third quarter just ripe for ringing, *ring-fähig* if I may use a German term which has no exact equivalent in English, and for the last quarter too advanced in age to be ringed with safety. Young birds that leave the nest almost at birth are in a different category from young song-birds, and most of them can be ringed at any time they can be caught. Young ducks, however, must not be ringed when they are very small and fairly easily caught, as their legs are still too small, but by the time their legs have grown big enough for the ring not to slip off, they are almost able to fly.

When confronted by a nestful of young birds judged of ringable age, it is a good plan to remove the entire brood from the nest and place them in a dark cloth bag (*not* your cap or

6

other item of clothing, as young birds removed from the nest have a tiresome nervous habit of defecating). If you can place something over the nest to prevent the parent bird seeing that it is empty, so much the better. Most ringers work out their individual technique of handling nestlings for ringing, but one very good plan is to hold the bird in the left hand with its back against the palm and its head beneath the wrist, so that the left leg can be controlled by holding the tarsal joint (the 'knee') between the thumb and the forefinger. If the bird is to be ringed with a No. 1 ring (which should have previously been prepared in a spiral, with one end curled inwards to a size slightly thicker than a small bird's leg) you then slip the ring on to the tarsus (the part of the leg between the 'knee' and the toes, and gently press the inside end of the ring to meet the inside surface of the ring on the far side of the bird's leg, so as to enclose the leg in a small metal sheath loose enough to allow it to slide about, but tight enough to stop it slipping off. The rest of the ring should then be carefully rolled round the sheath to form a cylinder, and the outside end pressed firmly down to make sure that there are no projecting corners that might catch in the grass or the nest lining. This is the process known as overlapping, and should only be used where explicitly stated. In all other cases the ring is fitted round the leg by simply meeting the two ends, but still taking care not to leave any sharp corners or gaps in which extraneous matter might catch.

The nestlings should be replaced *one at a time* either as they are ringed or after the whole brood has been ringed, according to local convenience. Care should be taken, not only to settle each one in before another is put on top of it, but to prevent any ringed leg protruding from the nest, as parent birds are liable to mistake the rings for faecal sacs, and attempt to remove them, with unhappy results.

Incidentally, if you have any choice in the matter, always ring nestlings between 1 and 4 in the afternoon, when they are at their drowsiest.

7

THE BIRDS IN THE BOOK

FULL TREATMENT in the text is accorded to the 183 birds which breed regularly in some part or other of the British Isles, and also to half a dozen (golden oriole, hoopoe, spotted crake, black-tailed godwit, black-necked grebe and Kentish plover), which are fairly frequent or increasing irregular breeders. Two birds in this total of 189 will not be found in any other standard work on British birds or their eggs (except *The Pocket Guide to British Birds*). They are the London pigeon, which frequents almost every town in the British Isles, even in such an out-of-the-way place as Mallaig, but is cold-shouldered by all other writers on birds, and the mandarin duck, which has established itself so firmly in several districts that it is bound to be accorded a place in time even in the most conservative and orthodox volumes.

Briefer treatment is given to nineteen species which have bred in Britain on only a very few occasions; to two (bee-eater and Temminck's stint) which have attempted to breed but have failed to bring off any young; to two introduced species (Carolina duck and Egyptian goose) which are established in one or two very limited areas; to eight which formerly bred regularly but no longer do so, and which may or may not return as the bittern and avocet have already done; to two (serin and eastern collared dove) which are spreading on the Continent and may well begin breeding here in the next few years; and finally to thirteen species which have at some time or other been suspected of breeding, but never proved to do so, viz., firecrest, melodious warbler, woodchat, great black woodpecker, little crake, jack-snipe, purple sandpiper, turnstone, little bittern, goldeneye, king-eider, velvet-scoter and great northern diver. Since such suspicions may arise again, it is desirable to have brief details of what an ampler age used to call their 'nidification' available for information. Some of these details are not

8

available in many standard works on British birds. It seems probable, for instance, that some breeding records of the green sandpiper and the goldeneye have been missed because the people who might have been able to verify them did not know that the sandpiper nests in other birds' old nests and the duck in holes in trees.

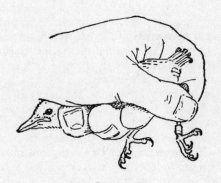

HOW TO HOLD A NESTLING FOR RINGING

HOW TO USE THE BOOK

AS IN *The Pocket Guide to British Birds* I have abandoned the systematic scientific classification of birds, which is apt to be confusing to bird-watchers in their early stages, in favour of a simpler system based on habitat and size. I am strengthened in this decision, not only by the favourable reception of this simpler system by readers of the earlier book, but by the fact that in the interval the scientific systematic classification has been turned upside down by the general adoption of the so-called Wetmore order. These *bouleversements* take place every twenty or thirty years: Harting in 1872 began with the birds of prey and ended with the petrels; Saunders in 1899 began with the thrushes and ended with the petrels; Witherby in 1919 began with the crows and ended with the game-birds; and now the *Popular Handbook* begins with the divers and ends with the finches. Who knows what will happen by 1984? At least there is every reason to suppose that the goldcrest will still be the smallest British bird and the mute swan the largest. (Of course, I would not advocate the simpler system for a book addressed to scientific ornithologists, but this one is meant for the bird-watcher in the street.) The system here adopted is first to divide the birds into three broad habitat groups (Land, Water-side, Water), and within each habitat group to set the birds out in ascending order of size in eight main groups based on the overall length of the bird. The text thus constitutes a broad identification key in itself, for if the nest of, say a small land bird about the size of a sparrow is seen, all the likely birds will be found within a few pages of each other.

SOME DEFINITIONS

Throughout the text the words 'British' or 'in the British Isles' must be understood as qualifying every statement, and any comparative statements must be taken as comparing only with other birds mentioned in the book. Further, no account has been taken of habits or habitats outside the breeding season, so that all statements must be taken as referring to the breeding season, unless it is expressly stated otherwise.

NAMES

English names are the same as those in *The Pocket Guide to British Birds*, and differ from those in other standard works to the minor extent there indicated. Under each species a page-reference to *The Pocket Guide to British Birds* (abbreviated PGBB) has been given. Scientific names follow the British Ornithologists' Union's *Check-list of the Birds of Great Britain and Ireland* (1952), and therefore differ in some respects from those in *The Handbook of British Birds*.

THE HABITAT GROUPINGS

The three main categories used throughout the book are defined as follows:

LAND: Found predominantly on land away from water.
WATERSIDE: Generally found in the neighbourhood of water, but not normally swimming on it.
WATER: Normally flying over and swimming on water.

All water birds and many land birds may, of course, be seen temporarily at the water's edge. In this book these habitat groupings must be taken to apply to the birds, and not to their nests, since only a very few species actually have floating nests.

THE LENGTH GROUPS

Within each habitat grouping the birds are arranged in eight length groups, as nearly as possible in ascending order of size, starting with the smallest and ending with the largest. Thus the land birds start with the smallest British bird, the goldcrest, and end with the largest land bird, a scarce vagrant, the white stork, which has bred in Britain only once. The eight groups are based on the overall length of the bird from the tip of the bill to the tip of the tail, and each is represented by a common bird, as follows:

Length Groups

Length Group	Type Bird
1. Very Short	Blue Tit
2. Short	House-sparrow
3. Medium Short	Starling
4. Medium	Lapwing
5. Medium Long	Rook
6. Long	Mallard
7. Very Long	Cock Pheasant
8. Huge	Mute Swan

Where cock and hen birds differ significantly in size, as in the pheasant, the bird appears in the text in the position belonging to the smaller sex, usually the hen, but where immature birds are markedly shorter than the adults, as with the skuas, the bird appears in the position belonging to the adult. In *The Pocket Guide to British Birds* there are many cross-references in the text where birds overlap two size-groups or two habitat groupings, but these have been dispensed with in the present book.

HABITAT AND RANGE

This section is based very largely on PGBB, excluding information not relating to the breeding season. All statements as to habitat and range should therefore be taken as qualified by the phrase 'in the breeding season'. The term 'Resident' is used when a species is present throughout the year, whether or not the same individual birds are present. Many birds, like the song-thrush and linnet, are in fact partial migrants, though some are to be seen in every month of the year.

NEST

Nest sites should be regarded as normal or average ones; exceptions are given where practicable, but some birds, such as the pied wagtail, are so catholic in their choice of site that it is impossible to be comprehensive. A 'colonial' bird is taken as one that nests regularly in colonies close together; a 'social' bird is one that nests in looser aggregations, often several yards apart. Singleton nests of both colonial and social birds should always be reckoned with. A 'hollow' is a natural depression in the ground; a 'scrape' is a depression made by the bird. Some species are very constant in their choice of nest materials, others use whatever lies close at hand; for these latter the term 'local materials' is used. With ducks and geese the down and feathers used by the bird in lining the nest are valuable aids to identification, and specimens should always be taken if a duck's nest is found in the absence of its owner.

EGGS AND YOUNG

The figure immediately following '*Eggs*' is the average or normal number of eggs in the clutch. In a great many species this is variable, and both smaller and larger clutches than the figure given may be found. There is a general tendency for clutch-size to increase as the season advances, reach a peak and then decline. The shape of eggs is to be considered as ovoid or like that of the domestic fowl unless otherwise stated, i.e. blunter at one end than at the other. The length of the incubation period is also highly variable in most species, and the figure given is only an average; both sexes take part in incubation except where otherwise stated (this may be of help in identifying the bird where the sexes differ in plumage). In the description of the nestling, only the presence, not the absence, of spots on tongue or mouth is indicated. The fledging period is just as variable as the incubation period. The ring number (see p. 5) is given for each species. The term 'overlapped' is explained on p. 7. Certain species may not be ringed as nestlings because of the danger of damaging the nest in removing the brood; others, such as game-birds, may not be ringed at all, because they are non-migratory, often live under artificial conditions, and are habitually shot. The term 'chick' is used instead of 'nestling' where the young bird leaves the nest within two or three days of hatching.

SEASON

This is defined as the period during which either eggs or young may be found in the nest. It is thus much shorter for birds whose young leave the nest after a few hours than for birds with a long nestling period. Birds are single-brooded unless otherwise stated. 'Second broods' refer to genuine second broods after a first one has been safely reared. Many so-called second broods are merely repeats after the first brood has come to grief. In the latter part of the breeding season given here, therefore, the majority of occupied nests will be repeats, so that they will be much scarcer than in the early part. With many birds the breeding season is variable, and with most species occasional nests may be found outside the period indicated here. Freak autumn nests are found from time to time with many of the commoner birds.

A NOTE ON THE ILLUSTRATIONS

THE ILLUSTRATIONS are arranged in key form, according to the sites of the nests. Several birds that have more than one typical nest site are shown more than once, but no attempt has been made to illustrate uncommon or freak nest sites. Nor has any attempt been made to illustrate the habitat as distinct from the immediate surroundings of the nest. All birds that nest regularly in the British Isles are illustrated in colour, with the exception of a group of sea-birds with black-and-white plumages on plates 41 and 42. All birds that are certainly known to have nested in the British Isles are shown either in colour or in black-and-white. The majority of the birds included briefly in the text because they have been suspected of breeding in the past, or may be expected to do so in the future, have also been shown in black-and-white; the only exceptions are three birds of which the female is hardly distinguishable from a commoner bird, viz. melodious warbler (icterine warbler), Carolina duck (mandarin duck), king-eider (common eider).

All birds are drawn approximately to scale on each plate. Females only are shown, except where incubation is predominantly or exclusively by the male. This, together with the fact that by the spring many birds are less brightly plumaged than immediately after their moult the previous autumn, accounts for the somewhat dowdy appearance of many of the birds. Nestlings (at about one day old) have been shown for birds that leave the nest soon after hatching, and for a few other species, such as the auks, that have no proper nest. Two conventions that conflict with natural conditions have had perforce to be adopted. One is that well-hidden nests are shown opened up far enough to reveal the eggs (with domed nests and nests in holes, however, the egg appears in a 'box' outside). The other is that eggs and chicks are shown together, and in some cases an egg is shown on the edge of a nest being brooded by a bird, which would not of course occur in the wild.

DESCRIPTIONS OF NESTS
AND EGGS

For the plan of arrangement, and detailed notes on general points relating to the sub-headings under each bird, see pp. 10–14. If you want to find any particular bird quickly, use the index.

LAND BIRDS: Very Short

GOLDCREST *Regulus regulus* Plate 33   Kinglet Family *PGBB*, p. 16, plate 1

HABITAT AND RANGE. Woods, large gardens, churchyards and other places with scattered trees, especially yews and other conifers. Partial migrant, breeding almost throughout British Isles.

NEST. Habitually well concealed and suspended 3–50 feet up under far end of branch of conifer; sometimes in ivy against tree-bole or in tangle; rarely in evergreen or deciduous tree or bush. The only tiny round (but not domed) nest of moss and gossamer that is fastened to branch by handles; lined with feathers.

EGGS AND YOUNG. *Eggs:* 7–10; white or pale ochreous yellow, finely spotted brown at big end; incubation 15–16 days, by hen only. *Nestling:* Down sparse and greyish, mouth bright orange, gape pale pinkish; leaves nest at about 19 days. Not to be ringed as nestling.

SEASON. Mid-April to June; two broods.

FIRECREST (*Regulus ignicapillus*), Plate 47; Kinglet Family (*PGBB*, p. 16, plate 1). Much as goldcrest, but less strictly confined to conifers and eggs have warm pink hue. Annual winter visitor in very small numbers, mainly to S and E coastal counties; said to have bred Lancashire 1927, and does so regularly just across the Channel in France.

WREN *Troglodytes troglodytes* Plates 29, 37 Wren Family
PGBB, p. 17, plate 3

HABITAT AND RANGE. Almost universal on land, with preference for areas of low scrub, brambles and bushes. Resident
throughout British Isles.

NEST. A wide variety of low sites; typically in low bushes or
ivy against trees or walls, but often also in banks, haystacks,
holes, crevices and under rocks or tree-roots; less often in
nest-boxes and old nests of other birds. Height usually 3–5
feet, rarely over 6 feet. Nest domed in open sites, with round,
often tightly woven entrance; made of moss, dead grass and
leaves, bracken and other local materials. Each cock makes
several nests, of which only one is lined with feathers by hen
and used for brood.

EGGS AND YOUNG. *Eggs:* 5–6; white, speckled often sparsely
and chiefly at big end with brownish red; incubation 14–15
days, by hen only. *Nestling:* Down sparse and grey-black;
mouth bright yellow, gape pale yellow; leaves nest at about
16 days. Not to be ringed as nestling.

SEASON. Mid-April to July; two broods.

WILLOW-WARBLER *Phylloscopus trochilus* Plate 10
PGBB, p. 17, plate 1   [Warbler Family

HABITAT AND RANGE. Woods, heaths, commons, orchards,
large gardens, and other well-timbered and bushy places.
Summer visitor, breeding almost throughout British Isles.

NEST. Normally on the ground, often in a hollow, concealed
by grass, bracken or other herbage; occasionally a few feet
up in a low bush or ivy, and exceptionally much higher.
Entrance hole of domed nest is never tightly woven as wren's
often is; made of moss, dried grass and various local
materials, and usually lined with feathers.

EGGS AND YOUNG. *Eggs:* 6–7; white, occasionally unspotted
but usually marked with fine reddish spots, larger dark brown
spots, or pale reddish-brown blotches; incubation 13 days,
by hen only. *Nestling:* Down sparse and whitish; mouth
orange-yellow, with two faint brownish marks on tongue-

c   17

spurs; gape yellow; leaves nest at about 14 days. Ring number 1 overlapped.

SEASON. Last week of April to mid-July; sometimes two broods.

CHIFFCHAFF *Phylloscopus collybita* Plate 29
PGBB, p. 18, plate 1   [Warbler Family

HABITAT AND RANGE. Prefers more well-timbered areas than willow-warbler, needing both trees at least 15 feet high to sing from and thick undergrowth to nest in; especially fond of brambly fringes of woods. Summer visitor, but local in Scotland and very rarely N of Firth of Forth.

NEST. Usually in bramble-brake, butcher's broom, sedge tussock or other low bush or herbage, sometimes in deep shade; unlike willow-warbler very rarely actually on ground, but equally rarely more than a foot or two above it. Nest domed like willow-warbler's, but has more horizontal, slit-like entrance-hole and is less compactly built and more plentifully lined with feathers than that species; can also usually be told from both willow-warbler's and wren's by foundation of dead leaves. Much more loosely built than wren's, and never has tightly woven entrance-hole.

EGGS AND YOUNG. *Eggs:* 5–6; rather shiny white, usually with spots and freckles of purplish- or reddish-brown; incubation 13 days, by hen only. *Nestling:* Down sparse and greyish, shorter than willow-warbler; mouth dull yellow and, unlike willow-warbler, with no tongue-spots; gape pale yellow; leaves nest at 14 days. Ring number 1 overlapped.

SEASON. Late April to end June; often two broods in S.

COAL-TIT *Parus ater* Plates 1, 5   Tit Family
PGBB, p. 18, plate 2

HABITAT AND RANGE. Woods and places with scattered trees, especially conifers; more local and, except among conifers, much less common than great and blue tits. Resident almost throughout British Isles.

NEST. Always in a hole, in tree, stump, wall, bank or ground; usually lower than 4 feet, but occasionally much higher; will use nest-boxes freely. Nest a thick pad of animal hair or down, sometimes with feathers, on a foundation of moss.

EGGS AND YOUNG. *Eggs:* 7–10; white, usually more or less thickly spotted or speckled with reddish-brown; hidden under lining of nest until incubation begins; incubation 12–14 days, mainly by hen. *Nestling:* Down greyish; mouth orange-pink; gape pale yellow; leaves nest at 16 days. Ring number 1 overlapped.

SEASON. Mid-April to mid-June; second brood rare.

CRESTED TIT *Parus cristatus* Plate 3   Tit Family
PGBB, p. 19, plate 2

HABITAT AND RANGE. Resident; confined to pine forests in the Highlands of Scotland, chiefly in the Spey valley.

NEST. Invariably in a hole, usually an irregular one excavated or adapted by hen in a rotten pine-stump, but alders and birches also used and sometimes wooden or even iron fence-posts or holes in ground. Height usually under 10 feet, but occasionally much higher. Nest a thick pad of deer and other animal hair, wool and feathers, on a foundation of moss.

EGGS AND YOUNG. *Eggs:* 5–6; closely resemble tree-creeper's (below), but can be distinguished by absence of any reddish shell-marks; outstanding among tits' eggs for their bold blotches; hidden under nest-material during laying period; incubation about 14 days, by hen only. *Nestling*: Down dark grey; mouth dull yellow inside; gape brighter but paler yellow; leaves nest at 17–18 days. Ring number 1 overlapped.

SEASON. Late April to end May.

BLUE TIT *Parus caeruleus* Plate 5   Tit Family
PGBB, p. 19, plate 2

HABITAT AND RANGE. Woods, copses, gardens, orchards, town parks and squares, and other places with scattered trees. Resident throughout British Isles, but scarce and local in NW Scotland.

NEST. Almost invariably in a hole, usually in a tree, but often

In a wall or building, or in a nest-box; occasionally in a bank or old nest of other bird; freak sites such as letter-boxes not uncommon. Height almost anything from ground-level upwards. Nest a thick pad of hair, wool or feathers on a foundation of moss and dried grass; sometimes decorated with greenery during incubation.

EGGS AND YOUNG. *Eggs:* 8–15; white, usually well freckled with reddish-brown; hidden under nest-lining until incubation begins; incubation about 14 days, by hen only. *Nestling:* Down sparse and whitish; mouth dull orange-red inside; gape pale yellow; leaves nest at about 19 days. Ring number 1 overlapped.

SEASON. Nest-building from late March in some years; eggs and young April to mid-June; second broods very rare.

MARSH-TIT *Parus palustris* Plate 3   Tit Family
PGBB, p. 20, plate 2

HABITAT AND RANGE. Woods, copses and places with scattered trees, except town parks and gardens. Resident throughout England and Wales, but local in N Wales and extreme SW and N England, extending into Berwickshire.

NEST. Nearly always in natural hole in tree or stump, from almost ground-level to 20 feet or more; occasionally in excavated hole, hole in wall or nest-box. Nest a thick pad of animal hair or fur on a foundation of moss.

EGGS AND YOUNG. *Eggs:* 7–8; white, usually with reddish-brown spots; covered by nest-lining during laying period; incubation 13 days, by hen only. *Nestling:* Down sparse and grey-brown; mouth yellowish-brown; gape pale yellow; leaves nest at 15–16 days. Ring number 1 overlapped.

SEASON. Late April to early June; perhaps occasionally a second brood.

WILLOW-TIT *Parus atricapillus* Plate 3   Tit Family
PGBB, p. 20, plate 2

HABITAT AND RANGE. Woods, copses and places with scattered trees, usually well away from human settlements; often but by no means always near water. Resident throughout Great

Britain N to Inverness-shire, but rather local except in parts of N and SE England.

NEST. Round cavity excavated by bird in rotten tree-stump, bough or post, anything from 2 to 20 feet up, but mostly below 10 feet; birch, willow, elder and alder are most favoured trees; use of natural hole quite exceptional. Unlike woodpeckers, excavating birds drop their chips some way from the nest-hole. Nest much slighter than marsh-tit's, and rarely has moss in foundation, which is usually of wood-fibre or chips, surmounted by a thin pad of rabbit fur and often feathers.

EGGS AND YOUNG. *Eggs:* 5–9; similar to but rather brighter than marsh-tit's (above); covered by nest-material during laying period; incubation, by hen only, 13–14 days. *Nestling:* Similar to marsh-tit; leaves nest at about 17 days. Ring number 1 overlapped.

SEASON. Mid-April to June.

SERIN (*Serinus canarius*), Plate 47; Finch Family (*PGBB*, p. 21, plate 12). Much as goldfinch (below), but more associated with street trees and less so with fruit-trees. Vagrant, but has spread NW in Europe during past century and now breeds all along Channel and N Sea coasts from France to Denmark, so may well try to colonise SE England, and should be listened for in well-timbered urban areas in spring.

GOLDFINCH *Carduelis carduelis* Plate 33 Finch Family *PGBB*, p. 22, plates 11, 12

HABITAT AND RANGE. Neighbourhood of human settlements, especially orchards, large gardens, parks, thick hedgerows and open woodland. Resident, but local in some areas, especially in Scotland, and absent from much of Highlands.

NEST. Well concealed in a tree or tall bush, often a fruit-tree and towards the end of a bough; usually 6–25 feet up. Nest a very neat cup of moss and various animal and vegetable fibres, lined with thistledown and wool.

EGGS AND YOUNG. *Eggs:* 5–6; bluish-white, rather sparsely

spotted and streaked purplish-red; incubation by hen only, 12–13 days. *Nestling:* Down dark grey; mouth purplish above, red below; gape creamy white; leaves nest at 13–14 days. Ring number 1 overlapped.

SEASON. May to July or August; two broods, occasionally three.

SISKIN *Carduelis spinus* Plate 33   Finch Family
PGBB, p. 22, plate 12

HABITAT AND RANGE. Open pinewoods, and places with scattered coniferous trees, including large gardens. Resident, local in Scottish Highlands, Ireland, and on either side of Solway Firth, occasionally breeds in South.

NEST. Invariably (except in cases of escaped cage-birds) in a coniferous trees, especially pine, spruce and larch; height anything from 15 feet to upper limit of tree growth, often towards the end of a bough. Nest similar to goldfinch (above), but smaller and neater.

EGGS AND YOUNG. *Eggs:* 4–5; similar to goldfinch (above), but bluer; incubation by hen only, about 11 days. *Nestling:* No description available; leaves nest at about 15 days. Ring number 1 overlapped.

SEASON. April–May (Ireland) and May–June (Scotland); two broods.

LESSER REDPOLL *Carduelis flammea* Plate 31 Finch
PGBB, p. 23, plates 10,11   [Family

HABITAT AND RANGE. Heaths, bogs and copses with birch and alder, also among conifers and in large gardens and shrubberies. Resident, but local, especially in England and Wales.

NEST. Often social. In trees and bushes at all heights from 2–3 feet upwards. Can be told from all other finch nests, except bullfinch, by foundation of thin twigs, which, with ends of bents, etc. sticking out higher up, make it look rather untidy outside. Inside is a neat, goldfinch-like cup, lined with willow-down, hair and feathers.

EGGS AND YOUNG. *Eggs:* 4–6; rather deep matt blue, bluer than any other finch's except bullfinch, with pale brown spots

and streaks; incubation by hen only, 10–11 days. *Nestling:*
Down dark grey; mouth red with two pale spots on roof;
gape yellow; leaves nest at about 11–12 days. Ring number 1
overlapped.
SEASON. May to July or August; sometimes two broods.

TREE-CREEPER *Certhia familiaris* Plate 3 Creeper Family
PGBB, p. 24, plate 4
HABITAT AND RANGE. Woods, copses, and places with scattered
trees, such as parks and gardens. Resident almost throughout British Isles.
NEST. Normally behind loose bark or ivy roots on tree-trunks,
or in other crevices in trees; fond of oaks or elms struck by
lightning; exceptionally in crevices in walls or old wooden
sheds. Can be induced to nest in specially designed nest-
boxes. Nest made of dried grass, roots and various other
local materials, lined with feathers, wool, etc. Tell-tale
pieces of nest material usually stick out of cracks in bark.
EGGS AND YOUNG. *Eggs:* 6; white with red-brown spots mostly
at thick end, and reddish-purple shell-marks which distinguish them from crested tit's; incubation about 15 days.
Nestling: Down abundant and dark grey; mouth yellow;
gape yellowish; leaves nest at 14–15 days. Ring number 1
overlapped.
SEASON. Mid-April to June; sometimes two broods.

PIED FLYCATCHER *Muscicapa hypoleuca* Plate 5
PGBB, p. 24, plates 4, 5, 16   [Flycatcher Family
HABITAT AND RANGE. Woods, especially in hill country, parks,
gardens and orchards. Summer visitor to parts of Wales, N
and W England and W Scotland, but spreading and might
occur anywhere W of a line from Hull to Lyme Regis.
NEST. Always in a hole, normally in a tree, but sometimes in
a wall or building, at almost any height, but usually 3–20
feet; readily uses nest-boxes. Nest commonly with foundation of oak-leaves and vegetable fibres, especially honeysuckle, lined with grasses, fibres and other local materials.
EGGS AND YOUNG. *Eggs:* 6–8; pale blue; incubation by hen

only, 12–13 days. *Nestling:* Down sparse and dark grey; mouth orange-yellow; gape pale yellow; leaves nest at 13–14 days. Ring number 1 overlapped.

SEASON. Late April to June; sometimes two broods.

WOOD-WARBLER *Phylloscopus sibilatrix* Plate 10
PGBB, p. 25, plate 1   [Warbler Family

HABITAT AND RANGE. Woods, especially those with sparse undergrowth, such as beechwoods on chalk or limestone, and valley oakwoods and birchwoods in Wales and W Scotland. Summer visitor, throughout Great Britain, but rather local in S and E England, Midlands and NW Scotland; very scarce and local in Ireland.

NEST. Always in a natural hollow in the ground, with dome showing above; often but by no means always under cover. Nest made of dried grass and other local materials, lined with finer grass and hair, but unlike willow-warbler never with feathers.

EGGS AND YOUNG. *Eggs:* 5–7; white, thickly spotted with dark red-brown and sometimes with ashy shell-marks; incubation by hen only, 13 days. *Nestling:* Down sparse and pale grey; mouth bright yellow; gape pale yellow; leaves nest at 11–12 days. Ring number 1 overlapped.

SEASON. Mid-May to June; very occasionally two broods.

GRASSHOPPER-WARBLER *Locustella naevia* Plate 30
PGBB, p. 25, plate 3   [Warbler Family

HABITAT AND RANGE. Heaths, commons, marshes, sites of felled woodland, osier-beds, and other places, both damp and dry, with scattered bushes, brambles and coarse vegetation. Summer visitor, local; absent from N Scotland.

NEST. Always on the ground or a few inches above it; very well-concealed in brambles, tussock of grass or sedge, or similar tuft of thick vegetation, approached by a covered run. Made of and lined with dried grasses on a foundation of dead leaves or of reed-blades lined with reed-flowers.

EGGS AND YOUNG. *Eggs:* 6; creamy white, thickly speckled with reddish-brown; incubation about 14 days. *Nestling:*

Down greyish; mouth yellow with sides of roof olive-green, and two black spots at base and one at tip of tongue; leaves nest at about 11 days. Ring number 1 overlapped.

SEASON. Mid-May to July; two broods in S and sometimes in N.

DARTFORD WARBLER *Sylvia undata* Plate 28
PGBB, p. 26, plate 4   [Warbler Family

HABITAT AND RANGE. Sandy heaths and commons with tall heather or gorse, less often on gorsy downs. Resident but very local and chiefly on the Greensand, in S and SE England, with an outlying colony in Devon.

NEST. Usually in long heather or gorse, exceptionally in other bushes; 6 inches to 3 feet from ground. Usually compacter than common whitethroat's, and made mainly of heather or gorse with various other local materials; lined with down and other local materials, spiders' cocoons often woven into rim. Tends to be social when numerous.

EGGS AND YOUNG. *Eggs:* 3–4; whitish, sometimes tinged green, thickly speckled with varying shades of grey; incubation about 12 days. *Nestling:* No down; mouth pale yellow with two black spots on tongue; gape yellow; leaves nest at about 13 days. Ring number 1 overlapped.

SEASON. Late April to end June; two broods, perhaps occasionally three.

WHINCHAT *Saxicola rubetra* Plates 10, 28 Thrush Family
PGBB, p. 26, plates 5, 7, 10

HABITAT AND RANGE. All kinds of rough grassland, including hillsides, heaths, commons, marshes, water-meadows, waste ground and embankments; low bushes, tall plants or artificial song-posts are necessary. Summer visitor, breeding almost throughout British Isles; commonest in moorland areas of Wales, N England and Scotland; distinctly local in SE England, Cornwall, Ireland and Scottish isles.

NEST. Always on ground in rough herbage, sometimes under a low bush; often with access by a covered runway. Built mainly of dried grass, with thinner grasses and hair in lining.

EGGS AND YOUNG. *Eggs:* 5–7; deep greenish-blue, usually

finely speckled with rusty brown; incubation 13 days, by hen only. *Nestling:* Dark grey down, mouth orange-yellow, gape yellowish; leaves nest at about 13 days. Ring number 1 overlapped.

SEASON. Mid-May to mid-July; sometimes two broods.

STONECHAT *Saxicola torquata* Plates 10, 28
PGBB, p. 27, plates 5, 7, 10 [Thrush Family

HABITAT AND RANGE. Fond of gorsy places, such as heaths, commons, downland, hillsides and cliff-tops, but also frequents tall heather and rough grassland with young trees or low bushes. Resident throughout British Isles, but decreasing and local, especially in Midlands and SE England; commonest near the sea.

NEST. On or very near the ground, usually at the foot of a gorse or other bush, sometimes with access by a run. Built of and lined with dried grass and other local materials.

EGGS AND YOUNG. *Eggs:* 5–6; similar to whinchat's, but greener and much paler, also more decidedly freckled and often zoned with rusty brown; incubation by hen only, 14–15 days. *Nestling:* Similar to whinchat, but down sparser and mouth lacks orange tinge; leaves nest at 12–13 days. Ring number 1 overlapped.

SEASON. Last few days March till early August; two broods normal, three not uncommon in south.

HOUSE-MARTIN *Delichon urbica* Plate 39
PGBB, p. 27, plates 9, 65 [Swallow Family

HABITAT AND RANGE. Outskirts of large towns, country towns, villages, isolated farms and houses; also cliffs (sea and inland) and quarries. Summer visitor, almost throughout British Isles, but local in Ireland.

NEST. Colonial. Almost invariably affixed to outside wall of house or other building, immediately under eaves; in some districts also against bridges, cliffs or quarry-faces. Uniquely shaped among nests of British birds, like half a pudding-basin, the open side flat against the wall; access by a small slit at the top on one side. Made of gobbets of mud plastered together with dried grasses, and lined with straw, feathers and other local materials. Quite exceptionally placed inside a building, like swallow's.

EGGS AND YOUNG. *Eggs:* 4–5; white with slight gloss; incubation 14–15 days. *Nestling:* Down rather sparse, long and whitish; mouth yellow, gape pale yellow; leaves nest at about three weeks. Not to be ringed as nestling.

SEASON. Mid-May to early October; two or three broods.

HOUSE-MARTIN GATHERING MUD FOR
NEST

LAND BIRDS: Short

LINNET *Carduelis cannabina* Plates 28, 31   Finch Family
  PGBB, p. 28, plates 10, 11, 14
HABITAT AND RANGE. All kinds of bushy places, such as gorsy
  commons and heaths, gardens and rough or waste ground,
  also sand-hills and salt-marshes. Resident throughout
  British Isles, but very local in Scottish Highlands.
NEST. Tends to be social. In almost any kind of bush, hedge
  or low branch of tree, from about 1–10 feet high; occasionally
  in broccoli, shrubby seablite or other stout, low plant, or in
  ivy against tree-trunk. Made of dried grasses and other local
  materials, and lined mostly with hair and wool. Less bulky
  than greenfinch's.
EGGS AND YOUNG. *Eggs:* 4–6; bluish-white, pale to deep,
  rather sparsely spotted or streaked purplish-red; incubation
  about 11 days. *Nestling:* Down greyish, mouth pink, gape
  pale pink; leaves nest at 11–12 days. Ring number 1 overlapped. Often victimised by cuckoo.
SEASON. Mid-April to July or even August; two broods and
  sometimes three.

TWITE *Carduelis flavirostris* Plate 28   Finch Family
  PGBB, p. 28, plates 11, 14
HABITAT AND RANGE. Hills, moors, mosses and other rough
  open ground. Resident; very local in Pennines N from
  Staffordshire, rather more widely spread in S Scotland,
  common in W Highlands and islands of Scotland, and in
  Ireland (except central plain).
NEST. Tends to be social, with nests not far apart. In almost
  any kind of site on or within 2–3 feet of ground. Made of
  dried grass, wool (in lining) and other local materials.
EGGS AND YOUNG. *Eggs:* 5–6; similar to linnet's, but bluer and
  with fewer and bolder markings; incubation by hen only,
  12–13 days. *Nestling:* Down pale buffish-grey, mouth

28

pinkish-purple, gape whitish; leaves nest at about 15 days. Ring number 1 overlapped.

SEASON. Late April (Ireland) to early July; often two broods.

ICTERINE WARBLER (*Hippolais icterina*), Plate 43; Warbler Family (*PGBB*, p. 29). Scarce passage migrant, but has bred at least once (Wiltshire, 1907). Neatly built nest 4–8 feet up in fork of bush or hedge; eggs pinkish-white sparsely marked black.

MELODIOUS WARBLER (*Hippolais polyglotta*), Warbler Family (*PGBB*, p. 29). Passage migrant, much scarcer than icterine, but believed to have bred twice (Surrey, 1884; Sussex, about 1893), though eggs might have been icterine's. Nest similar to icterine's, but usually placed lower down, often near water; eggs very similar to icterine's.

LESSER WHITETHROAT *Sylvia curruca* Plate 29
PGBB, p. 30, plate 4   [Warbler Family
HABITAT AND RANGE. Similar to common whitethroat (below), but prefers places with more trees and taller hedges and bushes, such as shrubberies and large gardens. Summer visitor, not uncommon in S England, Midlands and E Wales, but local in N England and Isle of Man, and not at all in Cornwall, W Wales, Scotland and Ireland.

NEST. In all kinds of hedges, bushes, shrubs and bramble or briar brakes, usually 2–5 feet up, but exceptionally up to 10 feet; generally higher than common whitethroat's. Built and lined with rootlets, hair and various other local materials; may be decorated with spiders' cocoons; distinctly smaller, frailer and shallower than common whitethroat's and lacks its substantial base.

EGGS AND YOUNG. *Eggs:* 5; creamy white, boldly marked with sepia brown, suffused with lighter brown or grey, and often zoned; incubation 10–11 days. *Nestling:* No down; mouth orange-yellow, with black spot on each side of base of tongue; gape pale yellow; leaves nest at about 11 days. Ring number 1 overlapped.

SEASON. May to mid-July; often two broods.

COMMON WHITETHROAT *Sylvia communis* Plate 29
PGBB, p. 30, plate 3 [Warbler Family

HABITAT AND RANGE. Areas with tangled vegetation, including brambles, briars, bushes and hedgerows, especially heaths, commons, roadsides, clearings in and edges of woods. Summer visitor, common throughout British Isles; but local in N Scotland.

NEST. Low down in a bramble or briar brake, young thorn-bush or rough herbage such as rushes or nettles; usually within a foot or two of the ground, and only very exceptionally over 5 feet. Stouter than nests of other *Sylvia* warblers, especially at the base; made of dry grasses and similar local materials, nearly always lined with hair (usually black) and often decorated with pale fluffy objects.

EGGS AND YOUNG. *Eggs:* 4–5; highly variable, but usually with greenish or stone-coloured ground, and very diversely marked with spots, blotches and speckles in some shade of greenish-grey or greenish-black; incubation about 12 days. *Nestling:* No down; mouth pink at back, yellowish at front, with two dark spots on spurs and two more at tip of tongue; gape pale yellow; leaves nest at about 11 days. Ring number 1 overlapped. Sometimes victimised by cuckoo.

SEASON. May to late July; two broods normal.

GARDEN-WARBLER *Sylvia borin* Plate 29
PGBB, p. 30, plate 3 [Warbler Family

HABITAT AND RANGE. Clearings in woods, copses, felled woodland, commons, heaths, osier-beds, shrubberies, large (but not medium or small) gardens, and other places with plenty of brambles, briars and similar undergrowth. Summer visitor, common over most of England and Wales, but local in Scotland (not north of Highland line) and Ireland.

NEST. Low down in bushes (often rhododendrons), brambles or coarse vegetation; rarely above 3–4 feet and tends to be lower than blackcap's. Frail nest (but stouter than blackcap's) of dried grass and similar local materials, lined with rootlets, hair, etc. but not decorated on rim like blackcap's nor suspended by basket-handles.

30

EGGS AND YOUNG. *Eggs:* 4–5; variable, but usually whitish or greenish-white, with markings ranging from a few bold blotches to many faint frecklings of some more or less olive-brown colour; not certainly distinguishable from blackcap's; incubation 12 days. *Nesting:* No down, mouth dark orange-red with a pale purple spot on either side of base of tongue: gape whitish; leaves nest at 9–10 days. Ring number 1 over-lapped. Sometimes victimised by cuckoo.

SEASON. Mid-May to late June; perhaps sometimes two broods.

BLACKCAP *Sylvia atricapilla* Plate 29 Warbler Family
PGBB, p. 31, plates 3, 4

HABITAT AND RANGE. Similar to garden-warbler (above), but shows greater preference for shade and the presence of trees. Summer visitor, with range as garden-warbler, but breeds locally farther north in Scotland.

NEST. Site similar to garden-warbler's, but tends to be higher up and occasionally at 10 feet or more; often in elder and evergreens, especially box, snowberry and rhododendron. Nest like a slighter and neater garden-warbler's, but is supported by basket-handles and often has cocoons and other decorations on rim. Unlined cock's nests are sometimes made.

EGGS AND YOUNG. *Eggs:* 4–5; cannot certainly be told from garden warbler's, but tend to be slightly smaller and a pink variety is not uncommon; incubation varies from 10 to 15 days. *Nestling:* No down, mouth dull pink, with two faint brown oval spots on either side of base of tongue; gape whitish; leaves nest at 11–12 days. Ring number 1 over-lapped.

SEASON. Last days of April to mid-July; often two broods in south.

SPOTTED FLYCATCHER *Muscicapa striata* Plates 7, 37
PGBB, p. 31, plates 4, 5 [Flycatcher Family
HABITAT AND RANGE. Parks, gardens, riverside trees and the

edges of and clearings in woods; common in suburbs. Summer visitor, breeding almost throughout British Isles.

NEST. Always on a ledge of some kind, either in creeper on a wall, against a tree-trunk, on a bough or beam, in an old nest of another bird, in some sort of cavity in a wall or tree, or in a suitable nest-box; usually at a height of 5–15 feet. Rather untidily built of moss, wool, hair and other local materials, bound together with cobwebs. Same site may be used year after year.

EGGS AND YOUNG. *Eggs:* 4–5; very variable, ranging from greenish to bluish, either speckled all over or spotted mainly at big end with reddish-brown; incubation about 13 days. *Nestling:* Down grey and rather sparse, mouth orange-yellow, gape yellowish; leaves nest at 13–14 days. Ring number 1 overlapped.

SEASON. Mid-May to July; sometimes two broods, same nest being occasionally used for second brood.

COMMON REDSTART *Phoenicurus phoenicurus* Plates 1, 5
PGBB, p. 32, plates 5, 6   [Thrush Family

HABITAT AND RANGE. Woods, parks, orchards and other places with old trees, also open country with stone walls or quarries. Summer visitor, breeding almost throughout Great Britain, but absent Cornwall and Scottish Isles (except Mull), and local in Devon, SE England and Scotland. Absent from Ireland.

NEST. In a wide range of holes in trees, walls or quarries, from ground level to 12 or more feet up; also on ground in banks or among bracken or other vegetation; readily makes use of nest-boxes. Made of dried grass and other local materials, lined with hair and feathers.

EGGS AND YOUNG. *Eggs:* 5–8; blue, somewhat paler than hedge-sparrow's, and of a rather different shade; incubation by hen only, about 13 days. *Nestling:* Down longish and dark grey; mouth pale orange, gape yellowish; leaves nest at 15–16 days. Ring number 1 overlapped.

SEASON. Mid-May to June and July; two broods exceptional.

BLACK REDSTART *Phoenicurus ochruros* Plates **7, 39**
PGBB, p. 32, plates 5, 6, 33 [Thrush Family

HABITAT AND RANGE. Towns, near rubbly waste ground, such
as bombed and building sites, or lawns; also sea-cliffs.
Summer visitor, 20–30 pairs breeding annually in Central
London and in various coastal towns from Norfolk to
Sussex, and occasionally in industrial towns inland; non-
breeding cocks have occupied territories in towns as far W
and N as Cardiff, Liverpool and Edinburgh. Bred in
Cornwall 1927-39.

NEST. On a ledge or in a crevice, usually on or in a ruined
building, or on a cliff; sometimes in outhouse of inhabited
building, like swallow (beware occasional nest of common
redstart in such sites). Made of various local materials and
lined with hair and sometimes feathers.

EGGS AND YOUNG. *Eggs:* 4–5; glossy white; incubation by hen
only, about 13 days. *Nestling:* Long dark grey down, mouth
deep yellow, gape whitish; leaves nest at 16–17 days. Ring
number 1 overlapped.

SEASON. Late April to July; two broods, perhaps sometimes
three.

ROBIN *Erithacus rubecula* Plates **7, 10** Thrush Family
PGBB, p. 33, plates 5, 10

HABITAT AND RANGE. Always near cover, in woods, copses,
gardens, town parks and hedgerows; a common suburban
bird. Resident almost throughout British Isles, but local in
N Scotland.

NEST. Well hidden in a wide variety of sites from the ground
to 10 or more feet high, such as under thick herbage, on a
bank, in an ivied tree or wall, on a ledge in a shed, in a
haystack, or in an old food-tin, etc.; often in a nest-box.
Made largely of moss, usually on a foundation of dead
leaves, and lined with hair.

EGGS AND YOUNG. *Eggs:* 5–6; white, or pale greenish-blue,
but normally more or less suffused with reddish-brown
frecklings, which may completely obscure the ground-colour;
occasionally unmarked; incubation by hen only, 14 days.

D 33

Nestling: Long blackish down, mouth yellow, gape yellowish; leaves nest at about 14 days. Ring number 1 overlapped, but young should not be ringed after 9th day. Occasionally victimised by cuckoo.

SEASON. Late March to June or occasionally July (a good many winter nests on record, especially in February); two broods normal.

NUTHATCH *Sitta europaea* Plate 3   Nuthatch Family
PGBB, p. 34, plates 2, 20

HABITAT AND RANGE. Woods, copses and well-timbered parks and gardens; not in pure coniferous woods. Resident, fairly common in England and most of Wales, N to Humber and Mersey; local on E side N to SE Durham; absent from Isle of Wight.

NEST. Always in a hole, usually over 6 feet up in trees, occasionally in walls or buildings or even haystacks or old magpie's nests; will use nest-box. Mouth of nest-hole reduced in size with mud when necessary. Lining of flakes of bark (pine whenever possible) or dead leaves is used to cover eggs in bird's absence.

EGGS AND YOUNG. *Eggs:* 6-10; white, spotted with reddish-brown; incubation by hen only, 14–15 days. *Nestling:* Long dark grey down, mouth dark flesh-colour, gape ivory-white; leaves nest at about 24 days. Ring number 1A overlapped.

SEASON. Late April to June; perhaps occasionally a second brood.

GREAT TIT *Parus major* Plate 5   Tit Family
PGBB, p. 34, plate 2

HABITAT AND RANGE. All well-timbered places, such as woods, copses, parks, gardens and hedgerows; a common suburban bird. Resident and common throughout British Isles, but local in N and W Scotland.

NEST. Almost always in a hole, usually in a tree or stump, but often in a wall or building, or even in the ground; exceptionally in other birds' old nests or even openly in a hedgerow; commonly in nest-boxes. Made mostly of moss, lined with a thick felt of hair or down; eggs hidden in lining until incubation begins.

EGGS AND YOUNG. *Eggs:* 9–12; white, more or less heavily marked with red-brown; incubation by hen only, about 14 days. *Nestling:* Longish grey down, mouth orange, gape pale yellow; leaves nest at 18–20 days. Ring number 1 overlapped.

SEASON. Late April to June; occasionally a second brood.

LONG-TAILED TIT *Aegithalos caudatus* Plate 31
PGBB, p. 35, plates 2, 17   [Tit Family

HABITAT AND RANGE. Woods, copses, bushy heaths and commons, overgrown hedgerows. Resident and common almost throughout British Isles.

NEST. In trees, bushes and brakes at any height from 4 feet upwards; often in a gorse- or thorn-bush, but not uncommonly high up in the fork of a forest or orchard tree. Unmistakable domed, egg-shaped nest, with entrance-hole near top, is woven chiefly of moss and cobwebs, decorated outside with lichens and lined inside with anything from one thousand to two thousand feathers. Shape of nest gives rise to local name of 'bottle-tit'.

EGGS AND YOUNG. *Eggs:* 8–12; white, usually with reddish-brown freckling; incubation almost entirely by hen, about 16 days. *Nestling:* No down, mouth and gape yellow; leaves nest at 15–16 days. Not to be ringed as nestling.

SEASON. Nests begun in late February and March, when half-completed cups may often be seen; eggs in April; young fledge in May; normally one brood only.

TREE-SPARROW *Passer montanus* Plate 5 Sparrow Family
PGBB, p. 35, plate 15

HABITAT AND RANGE. All kinds of places with old and pollard trees, especially farmland, orchards, parks and large gardens, but sometimes in quite open country or even marine islands. Resident and widespread, but always local and especially so in Ireland and on W side of Great Britain.

NEST. Almost always in a hole in a tree, wall or building, usually over 4 feet up; also in haystacks, cliffs, quarries and other birds' nests; exceptionally openly in a thick hedge; often in nest-boxes. Construction and materials as house-sparrow (below). Beware occasional nests of house-sparrow in tree-holes and nest-boxes, also occasional nests of tree-sparrow in martin's nests.

EGGS AND YOUNG. *Eggs:* 5–7; very variable, white more or less heavily marked with grey, brown or dark chestnut (extremes are pure white and completely suffused with purple-brown markings); markedly smaller and glossier than house-sparrow's; one egg in each clutch usually paler than others; incubation about 13 days. *Nestling:* No down, mouth dull pink with dark spot sometimes at tip of tongue, gape yellow; leaves nest at about 13 days. Ring number 1 overlapped.

SEASON. Late April to August; two broods normal, three occasional.

HOUSE-SPARROW *Passer domesticus* Plates 7, 33
PGBB, p. 35, plates 14, 15   [Sparrow Family

HABITAT AND RANGE. Confined to occupied human settlements, from isolated farmsteads to centres of large cities. Resident and common throughout British Isles.

NEST. Usually colonial. Normally in a hole or crevice in a building, often under eaves, but also commonly in creeper on walls, trees, hedges and in other open sites; usually over 4 feet up; nests of house-martins often appropriated, also nest-boxes intended for other species. Untidy nest of dried grass, straw, etc. lined with feathers, is usually roughly domed when in the open, but may be very scanty in a hole; like tree-sparrow, site is often betrayed by straw sticking out of hole.

EGGS AND YOUNG. *Eggs:* 4–5; whitish, usually more or less heavily marked with grey or brown speckles; incubation about 13 days. *Nestling:* No down, mouth pinkish-yellow, gape pale yellow; leaves nest at 15 days. Ring number 1 overlapped.

SEASON. Collection of nest material normal in March, not infrequent late February; eggs from April onwards to

August; exceptionally eggs and young may be found in
autumn and winter; two broods, and often three.

GREENFINCH *Chloris chloris* Plate 31   Finch Family
   PGBB, p. 36, plate 12

HABITAT AND RANGE. All kinds of bushy places, mostly near
human settlements, such as gardens, shrubberies and thick
hedges. Resident and common almost throughout British
Isles.

NEST. Always in a bush, hedge, tree, or creeper on wall, rarely
below 4 feet or above 15 feet, sometimes in loose colonies.
Rather untidily made of dried grass, moss and often thin
twigs (sometimes foundation of twigs like bullfinch), lined
with hair, roots, and sometimes feathers. Stouter and untidier than linnet's, and not unlike neater hedge-sparrow's.

EGGS AND YOUNG. *Eggs:* 4–6; white or pale blue, usually
rather sparsely speckled reddish-brown; distinctly larger and
fatter than linnet's; incubation by hen only, 13–14 days.
Nestling: Rather long whitish down; mouth deep pink; gape
yellowish; leaves nest at 14–15 days. Ring number 1A
overlapped.

SEASON. Late April till July, with a few in August and September; two broods normal and sometimes three.

BULLFINCH *Pyrrhula pyrrhula* Plate 31   Finch Family
   PGBB, p. 37, plates 10, 11

HABITAT AND RANGE. Woods, copses, bushy places, overgrown
hedgerows, and large gardens. Resident and fairly common
throughout British Isles, but local in Scotland and Ireland.

NEST. Nearly always in a bush, hedge or brake, or in creeper
against a tree-trunk, usually from 2 to 6 feet up, but sometimes higher. Foundation always of fine twigs, and lining of
dark rootlets and hair, make nest a distinctive one.

EGGS AND YOUNG. *Eggs:* 5; greenish-blue, with rather sparse
purple-brown spots and streaks, mostly in a zone at the big
end; incubation about 13 days. *Nestling:* Longish grey
down, mouth pink with bright puce spots, gape pale yellow;
leaves nest at about 14 days. Ring number 1A overlapped.

SEASON. Late April to June, occasionally July to September; two broods normal, perhaps sometimes three.

BRAMBLING (*Fringilla montifringilla*), Plate 43; Finch Family (*PGBB*, p. 38, plates 14, 15). Has bred once certainly (1920) and very probably on two or three other occasions in N Scotland, and should be looked for there especially in birchwoods. Nest larger, untidier and usually at greater height than chaffinch's, and eggs tend to be darker and greener. Otherwise a widespread and not uncommon winter visitor.

CHAFFINCH *Fringilla coelebs* Plate 31 Finch Family
PGBB, p. 38, plates 10, 14

HABITAT AND RANGE. Wherever there are trees and bushes, in woods, copses, heaths, parks, gardens, farmland; common in suburbs. Resident and common throughout British Isles.

NEST. Almost always in a hedge, bush or tree, or against a tree-trunk; exceptionally on a ledge or a building; rarely below 4 feet or above 10 feet from ground, but sometimes as much as 60 feet up in forest trees. One of the neatest British birds' nests, moss and other local materials being carefully woven together, decorated externally with lichens and cobwebs, and lined with hair. Unlike any other finch nest except goldfinch's, but beware half-finished cups of long-tailed tit.

EGGS AND YOUNG. *Eggs:* 4–6; very variable, but usually greenish-blue or pale brown, with spots or streaks (often sparse) of purple-brown, the spots being usually surrounded by a pale cloudy 'penumbra'; occasionally unmarked; incubation almost entirely by hen, about 12 days. *Nestling:* Long pale grey down, mouth deep cerise with orange palate, gape white; leaves nest at 13–14 days. Ring number 1 overlapped.

SEASON. Mid-April to June; occasional second broods.

WHEATEAR *Oenanthe oenanthe* Plate 1 Thrush Family
PGBB, p. 39, plates 5, 7

HABITAT AND RANGE. All kinds of open, uncultivated country,

downs, hills, moors, mountains, cliffs, dunes, shingle, rabbit warrens. Summer visitor, breeding throughout British Isles, but local in Midlands and SE England.

NEST. In all kinds of holes in or near the ground, especially rabbit burrows, also in piles of stones and similar artificial sites. Made of dried grass and moss, lined with hair and various other local materials.

EGGS AND YOUNG. *Eggs:* 6; pale blue, occasionally faintly speckled dark red-brown; incubation about 14 days. *Nestling:* Long dark grey down, mouth pale orange, gape pale yellow; leaves nest at 15 days. Ring number 1 overlapped.

SEASON. Late April to June; two broods in some districts.

HEDGE-SPARROW *Prunella modularis* Plate 29
PGBB, p. 40, plates 4, 5 [Accentor Family

HABITAT AND RANGE. Places with bushes, scrub, bramble-brakes and similar undergrowth, such as gardens, copses, woods, heaths, hedgerows, cliffs, moorland cloughs; common in suburbs. Resident and common throughout British Isles.

NEST. In bushes, brakes, tangled vegetation and low trees, or in creeper against walls, at any height from 6 inches to 10 feet, but usually below 5 feet. Not unlike greenfinch's, but neater; made of moss and other local materials on a foundation of twigs; lined with hair, fur and wool.

EGGS AND YOUNG. *Eggs:* 4–5; blue; incubation by hen only, 12 days. *Nestling:* Longish black down, mouth bright orange with a black spot on each tongue-spur, gape pinkish; leaves nest at 12 days. Ring number 1 overlapped. Commonly victimised by cuckoo.

SEASON. Last few days March till July; normally two broods, occasionally three.

BARRED WOODPECKER *Dendrocopos minor* Plate 4
PGBB, p. 40, plate 16 [Woodpecker Family

HABITAT AND RANGE. All kinds of well-timbered country, open woodlands, heaths, farmland, parks, orchards, large gardens, much preferring broad-leaved to coniferous trees. Resident over most of England and Wales, but local in Yorkshire and W Wales, and rare in Lancashire and N England; absent from Scotland and Ireland.

NEST. Hole bored in decaying tree-trunk or branch at almost any height from ground; entrance slightly elliptical with height 1½ inch or a little more and breadth 1½ inch or a little less. Eggs repose on a few wood-chips.

EGGS AND YOUNG. *Eggs:* 5–6; glossy white, elliptical; incubation 14 days. *Nestling:* No down, mouth and gape flesh-coloured; leaves nest at about 3 weeks. Ring number 1A.

SEASON. Last days of April to June.

MEADOW-PIPIT *Anthus pratensis* Plate 11
PGBB, p. 41, plate 8   [Wagtail Family

HABITAT AND RANGE. Open, uncultivated country, moors, heaths, bogs, rough grazings, sandhills. Resident throughout British Isles, and especially common in N and W.

NEST. On the ground, in tussocks of grass or rushes, or among heather, always more or less sheltered from above, sometimes with a 'mouse-hole' entrance. Made of dried grass and other local materials, with some hair in lining.

EGGS AND YOUNG. *Eggs:* 4–6; very variable, but mostly whitish or brownish in ground-colour and fairly heavily speckled or suffused with ash-grey or earth-brown markings; incubation apparently by hen only, 13–14 days. *Nestling:* Longish grey-brown down, mouth carmine with whitish tongue-spurs, gape pale yellow; leaves nest at 13–14 days. Ring number 1 overlapped. Commonly victimised by cuckoo.

SEASON. Late April to July; two broods.

TREE-PIPIT *Anthus trivialis* Plate 11   Wagtail Family
PGBB, p. 42, plate 8

HABITAT AND RANGE. Places where scattered trees, poles or pylons provide song-posts, e.g. heaths, rough grazings, wood edges and clearings, railway cuttings and embankments, parkland. Summer visitor, common over most of Great

Britain, but thins out and does not breed in extreme W Cornwall or N Scotland; absent from Ireland.

NEST. On the ground, well hidden in grass or other vegetation, not necessarily close to a tree, sometimes with a 'mouse-hole' entrance. Made of dried grass on a foundation of moss, lined with grass and hair.

EGGS AND YOUNG. *Eggs:* 4–6; the most variable of any song-bird, but mostly some shade of reddish-brown, earth-brown or grey, much speckled, spotted or marbled with darker markings of the same colour; incubation by hen only, 13–14 days. *Nestling:* longish dark grey down, mouth orange with yellow edges and spurs of tongue and barbs of palate, gape pale yellow; leaves nest at 12–13 days. Ring number 1 over-lapped. Often victimised by cuckoo.

SEASON. May to early July; sometimes two broods.

WOOD-LARK *Lullula arborea* Plate 11   Lark Family
PGBB, p. 42, plate 8

HABITAT AND RANGE. Places with scattered trees, heaths, steep hillsides, parkland, felled woodlands, wooded combes and wood edges. Resident, breeding locally N to Flintshire and Yorkshire, but virtually absent from most of Midlands and relatively common only in parts of E Anglia and S England; an increasing species.

NEST. In a deep scrape in ground made by bird; often well concealed by low vegetation; may be approached by a run-way, less well defined than skylark's. Made of dried grass on foundation of moss, lined with finer grasses and hair.

EGGS AND YOUNG. *Eggs:* 3–5; greyish-white, well mottled with markings of various shades of reddish-brown, often zoned at big end; always redder than skylark's; incubation, apparently by hen only, about 14 days. *Nestling:* Dark grey down, mouth deep yellow with three black spots (one at tip of tongue and a small one on either side at base), gape yellowish; leaves nest at about 12 days. Ring number 1 overlapped.

SEASON. Late March to August; two broods normal, three occasional.

41

CIRL-BUNTING *Emberiza cirlus* Plate 28 Finch Family
PGBB, p. 44, plates 12, 15

HABITAT AND RANGE. Country with scattered trees and hedges, such as the borderland of downs and farmland, and large gardens on the edge of villages or small towns. Resident, breeding locally in all counties S of Thames, and even more locally in Wales and S Midlands.

NEST. Usually in a hedge or bush at about 3–6 feet, but also in a wide range of other sites, such as trees or on the ground. Rather untidy nest is bulkier than yellowhammer's and has foundation of moss.

EGGS AND YOUNG. *Eggs:* 3–5; similar to yellowhammer's (below), but often with greenish tinge and usually more heavily marked; incubation by hen only, about 12 days. *Nestling:* Long grey-brown down, mouth pink, gape yellow; leaves nest at about 12 days. Ring number 1 overlapped.

SEASON. Mid-May to August; two broods normal, three occasional.

YELLOWHAMMER *Emberiza citrinella* Plates 11, 28
PGBB, p. 44, plates 12, 13 [Finch Family

HABITAT AND RANGE. Hedges by roadsides and on farmland, bushy heaths and commons, edges of and clearings in woods; also in completely hedgeless farmland where artificial song-posts exist. Resident and common throughout British Isles.

NEST. Usually fairly well hidden either actually on the ground, on a bank or in a hedge-bottom, or else in a hedge, bush or brake or in ivy on a wall; but rarely above 4 feet. Made of dried grass and other local materials, lined with finer grass and hair; often betrayed by a long wisp protruding.

EGGS AND YOUNG. *Eggs:* 3–5; white, often with a purplish or reddish tinge, and marked with the characteristic brownish or purplish squiggles that have given rise to the local name of 'scribbling lark'; incubation about 13 days. *Nestling:* Longish grey down, mouth pink, gape pale yellow; leaves nest at 12–13 days. Ring number 1 overlapped. Occasionally victimised by cuckoo.

SEASON. Mostly May and June, but nests may be found from

April to August, or even September; two broods normal, sometimes three.

SNOW-BUNTING *Plectrophenax nivalis* Plate 1
PGBB, p. 96, plates 14, 16   [Finch Family
HABITAT AND RANGE. Barren, stony mountain-tops. Very local summer visitor to the Cairngorms and other high mountains in Scottish Highlands. Winter visitor elsewhere.
NEST. In a deep cavity among stones, scree or boulders. Made of dried grasses and other local materials, lined with feathers, etc.
EGGS AND YOUNG. *Eggs:* 4–6; bluish-, yellowish- or greenish-white, with a few reddish-brown spots and blotches, sometimes zoned at one end; incubation by hen only, 13–14 days. *Nestling:* Long dark grey down, gape yellow; leaves nest at about 11 days. Ring number 1 overlapped.
SEASON. Late May to July; sometimes two broods.

CROSSBILL *Loxia curvirostra* Plate 33   Finch Family
PGBB, p. 45, plates 10, 11, 12
HABITAT AND RANGE. Open coniferous woods, and scattered conifers on heaths, along roads and in parks. Resident and not uncommon in the central Scottish Highlands, also in the breck district of E. Anglia; breeds irregularly elsewhere following irruptions, most often on the heaths of Surrey, Hampshire, Berkshire and parts of Ireland.
NEST. Tends to be social. On the bough of a coniferous tree, usually over 10 feet. Substantial nest made of dried grass and other local materials, on a base of pine twigs, well lined with finer grass, hair and feathers.
EGGS AND YOUNG. *Eggs:* 4; so similar to greenfinch (above) that cannot be told apart even by experts; incubation by hen only, 12–13 days. *Nestling:* Dark grey down, mouth yellow and purplish-pink, gape pale yellow; leaves nest at 24 days or more. Ring number 1A.
SEASON. January to July, but most in February (England) and March (Scotland); perhaps sometimes a second brood.

HAWFINCH *Coccothraustes coccothraustes* Plate 33
  PGBB, p 45, plates 14, 15, 22   Finch Family
HABITAT AND RANGE. Woods and other well-timbered places,
  such as parks, gardens and orchards. Resident, widespread,
  but local in England and Wales (rare or unknown in northern
  and western extremities), mid and S Scotland; absent from
  rest of Scotland and from Ireland.
NEST. Tends to be social in some districts. Usually at a fair
  height in a tree, often a fruit-tree, and often near the end of
  a branch. Nest, with characteristic loose foundation of
  twigs and fibres, is rather skimpily made of roots, dried
  grasses, moss and lichen. Sometimes lined with hair, etc.;
  often decorated with sprigs of conifer.
EGGS AND YOUNG. *Eggs:* 4–5; ground-colour varies from pale
  blue or green to grey or buff, with a few bold sparse dark
  spots and markings; incubation about 12 days. *Nestling:*
  Long white down, mouth pink with reddish-purple at front
  of palate and spurs of tongue whitish, gape bright yellow;
  leaves nest at 12-13 days. Ring number 1A.
SEASON. Late April to June; sometimes two broods.

WRYNECK *Jynx torquilla* Plate 3   Woodpecker Family
  PGBB, p. 46, plate 17
HABITAT AND RANGE. All kinds of well-timbered country, from
  open woodlands, heaths and farmland to parks, orchards
  and large gardens; almost exclusively broad-leaved trees,
  with a special preference for old fruit-trees. Summer visitor,
  now breeding only very locally in SE England, mainly in
  Kent; has decreased in recent years.
NEST. Usually in a tree-hole, but more catholic than true
  woodpeckers, and will use a nest-box or almost any kind of
  hole in a wall, bank or thatched roof, or even a burrow; at
  almost any height, but often fairly low. Never excavates.
  No nest material.
EGGS AND YOUNG. *Eggs:* 7–10; dull white and almost elliptical;
  incubation 12 days. *Nestling:* No down, mouth and gape
  flesh-coloured, but gape paler; has a curious pad on the

44

'heel'; leaves nest at about 20 days. Ring number **1A** overlapped.

SEASON. May to July; two broods have been recorded.

NIGHTINGALE *Luscinia megarhyncha* Plate 10
  PGBB, p. 46, plates 3, 5, 6   [Thrush Family
HABITAT AND RANGE. All kinds of places where there are thickets, such as woods, copses, commons, heaths and over-grown hedgerows. Summer visitor, common in S England, but thinning out W to Devon, Glamorgan, lower Wye valley and Severn valley, and N to Shrewsbury, Trent valley and S Yorks.

NEST. Low down among rank vegetation, and often actually on the ground; usually very well hidden. Made and lined with dried grasses and hair on a foundation of dead leaves, often oak leaves.

EGGS AND YOUNG. *Eggs:* 5; dark olive-green or olive-brown; incubation by hen only, 13–14 days. *Nestling:* Grey-black down, mouth orange, gape whitish and yellowish; leaves nest at 11–12 days. Ring number 1 overlapped.

SEASON. May and June.

TAWNY PIPIT (*Anthus campestris*), plate 43; Wagtail Family (*PGBB*, p. 47, plate 8). Has bred at least once in Sussex (1905) and perhaps on other occasions, and should be looked for in sandy grassy places near the coast in SE England. Nest on the ground, eggs whitish with brown markings.

SWIFT *Apus apus* Plate 8   Swift Family
  PGBB, p. 47, plates 9, 66
HABITAT AND RANGE. Frequents mainly the neighbourhood of human settlements, but does not actually breed in the centres of the largest cities. Summer visitor, common throughout British Isles except NW Scotland.

NEST. Colonial. Usually in a crevice in a building (often under open eaves), but will also use holes or crevices in cliffs or quarries, nest-boxes and old house-martins' and house-sparrows' nests. Nest a shallow saucer made of agglutinated fragments of materials the bird finds floating in the air; the 'glue' is the bird's saliva.

EGGS AND YOUNG. *Eggs:* 2–3; dull white, elongated elliptical; incubation 18–19 days (but can be up to 24 days). *Nestling:* No down, mouth flesh-coloured with small pale brown spot at tip of tongue; gape whitish; leaves nest at any time from 35 to 56 days, but average about 42. Ring size SO.

SEASON. Late May to early August; one brood only.

RED-BACKED SHRIKE *Lanius collurio* Plate 32

PGBB, p. 48, plates 17, 31   [Shrike Family

HABITAT AND RANGE. Places with a scattered cover of thick bushes, such as commons, heaths and overgrown hedgerows. Summer visitor, not uncommon in parts of S and E England, but local elsewhere in England and Wales and very unusual N of Humber–Mersey line; absent from Scotland and Ireland.

NEST. Almost always in a thick bush or hedge, 4–6 feet up; some may be either higher or lower, occasionally in a small tree. Rather large and untidy nest is usually fairly conspicuous; made and lined with dried grass, hair and other local materials.

EGGS AND YOUNG. *Eggs:* 5–6; ground colour variable, either creamy or some shade of pale brown, pink or green, with brown or red-brown spots often zoned at big end; incubation almost entirely by hen, about 15 days. *Nestling:* No down, mouth orange-yellow, gape pale yellow; leaves nest at 14–15 days. Ring number 1A overlapped.

SEASON. Late May to early July.

WOODCHAT (*Lanius senator*), Plate 47; Shrike Family (*PGBB*, p. 49, plate 23). Said to have bred twice in Isle of Wight in nineteenth century, and as it breeds regularly only just across the Channel, might do so again. Nest often more substantial and usually at a greater height than red-backed shrike's (often at end of branch of olive or fruit-tree); eggs similar but usually tinged greenish and spotted grey-brown. Otherwise a scarce but increasing wanderer, especially in spring.

LAND BIRDS: Medium Short

CORN-BUNTING *Emberiza calandra* Plates 11, 28
  PGBB, p. 49, plate 13   [Finch Family

HABITAT AND RANGE. Open country, especially farmland and downland, and rough ground near the sea. Resident but local throughout the British Isles, in large scattered colonies; especially local in Scotland, Ireland and Wales.

NEST. Well hidden among coarse vegetation on or very near ground; sometimes under a clod in a cornfield or even a few feet up in a bush. Rather untidily made of dried grass and similar local materials.

EGGS AND YOUNG. *Eggs:* 3–5; greyish or pale brown with bold darker brown markings, which often include typical bunting-like squiggles; incubation 12–13 days, by hen only. *Nestling:* Long yellowish-buff down, mouth flesh-coloured, gape yellow; leaves nest at about 10 days. Ring number 1A overlapped.

SEASON. Begins late May, but mostly June and July, continuing exceptionally to September; two broods quite common.

SKYLARK *Alauda arvensis* Plate 11   Lark Family
  PGBB, p. 49, plate 8

HABITAT AND RANGE. Open country of all kinds, farmland, downland, moors and rough grazings, peat-bogs, mosses, estuarine marshes, sand-dunes. Resident and common throughout British Isles.

NEST. Always on the ground, in a scrape or a tuft of grass, among crops, in all kinds of grassland, on sand-dunes or even shingle. Made and lined with dried grass, often approached by a perceptible track.

EGGS AND YOUNG. *Eggs:* 3–4; whitish ground-colour normally scarcely visible through thick spotting and speckling of various shades of brown; incubation by hen only, 11 days. *Nestling:* Long pale yellow down, mouth dull yellow with two black spots at base of tongue and a third at the tip, gape white; leaves nest after 9–10 days. Ring number 1 overlapped.

SEASON. April to July; two broods regular, sometimes three.

PIED AND WHITE WAGTAILS *Motacilla alba* Plates 7, 39
PGBB, p. 50, plate 67   [Wagtail Family

HABITAT AND RANGE. Usually in or near human settlements, farms, villages and the outskirts of towns, more rarely in fully built-up areas; often, but by no means always, near water. Pied wagtail is resident almost throughout British Isles. White wagtail, the Continental form, has bred exceptionally in Fair Isle and several English counties.

NEST. One of the most catholic of all British birds in its choice of nest site, which is usually in some kind of cavity, or on a ledge, of a building, bank, stack, cliff or pile of stones, also in creeper or pollard tree, occasionally in the old nest of another bird. Made and lined with various local materials, such as moss and dried grass.

EGGS AND YOUNG. *Eggs:* 5–6; greyish-white, usually speckled or otherwise marked with grey or grey-brown; occasional clutches are hardly distinguishable from yellow or grey wagtails'; incubation 13–14 days. *Nestling:* Grey down, mouth orange-yellow, gape yellowish; leaves nest at 14–15 days. Ring number 1 overlapped. Commonly victimised by cuckoo.

SEASON. Mid-April to early August; two broods normal, three not uncommon.

QUAIL *Coturnix coturnix* Plate 12   Pheasant Family
PGBB, p. 52, plates 25, 71

HABITAT AND RANGE. Fields of growing crops, clover, lucerne and young corn, also in grass and rough tussocky grassland. Scarce and erratic summer visitor, breeding at times throughout British Isles, but more often on light calcareous soils of S England than elsewhere.

NEST. Always on ground among grass or crops, in a scrape lined with a few scraps of grass, etc.

EGGS AND YOUNG. *Eggs:* 7–12; buff, beautifully marbled with various shades of brown; incubation by hen only, about 19 days. *Chick:* Thickly covered with buff down, marbled black; leaves nest when a few hours old. Ring number 1A.

SEASON. Late May to July; sometimes two broods.

SWALLOW   *Hirundo rustica*   Plate 39   Swallow Family
PGBB, p. 52, plates 9, 65

HABITAT AND RANGE. In or near human settlements, including remote farms, but not in the centre of large cities. Summer visitor, breeding throughout British Isles, but local in NW Scotland.

NEST. Semi-social; usually on a ledge or rafter inside a building (especially farm buildings, outhouses and boat-houses), but sometimes in chimney-stacks and in some districts not uncommonly against walls without any support, like a house-martin's (but open above); exceptionally in quite natural sites such as cave-roofs. Flat, saucer-shaped nest is made of mud and dried grasses, lined largely with finer grass and feathers.

EGGS AND YOUNG. *Eggs:* 4–5; white, more or less heavily spotted or freckled red-brown; incubation by hen only, 14–17, mostly 15 days. *Nestling:* Longish grey down, mouth yellow, gape whitish; leaves nest at 18–23 days. Ring number 1 overlapped.

SEASON. Mid-May to early October; two broods normal, sometimes three.

STARLING   *Sturnus vulgaris*   Plate 6   Starling Family
PGBB, p. 55, plates 19, 69

HABITAT AND RANGE. Human settlements, including large towns, woods, parkland, sea-cliffs. Resident and common throughout British Isles, but local in N Scotland, W Wales and W Ireland.

NEST. Almost always in a hole, at almost any height, in a tree, building or cliff, also in quarries and nest-boxes; exceptionally in more open sites; often dispossesses woodpeckers. Untidy nest of straw, dried grass, feathers and other local

E   49

materials. Eggs are often dropped away from the nest and found lying on the ground.

EGGS AND YOUNG. *Eggs:* 5–7; pale blue; incubation 12–13 days. *Nestling:* Long greyish down, mouth bright yellow, gape pale yellow; leaves nest at about 21 days. Ring number 1A.

SEASON. April to June; occasionally in autumn and winter; sometimes two broods.

REDWING (*Turdus musicus*), Plate 32; Thrush Family (*PGBB*, p. 56, plates 18, 21). Has nested in Scotland more than a dozen times since 1926 and should be looked for, especially in birchwoods, in all parts of the Highlands. Nest like blackbird's (p. 54), and eggs very· like small blackbird's.

DOTTEREL *Charadrius morinellus* Plate 13 Plover Family *PGBB*, p. 56, plates 38, 42, 78, 82

HABITAT AND RANGE. Stony or tussocky mountain tops. Summer visitor, breeding in small numbers on the Cairngorms and a few other high mountains in Scotland, and perhaps still very sparingly indeed in N England.

NEST. In a scrape on the ground, usually among lichens, sometimes lined with moss, lichen, etc.; eggs often on a slight ridge.

EGGS AND YOUNG. *Eggs:* 3; ovoid, unlike most other waders; buffish, fairly thickly covered with dark brown blotches; incubation mainly by cock, 27–28 days. *Chick:* Thickly covered with cinnamon down, marbled black and whitish; leaves nest within a few hours. Ring number 2.

SEASON. Late May to early July.

LITTLE OWL *Athene noctua* Plates 1, 6, 40 Owl Family *PGBB*, p. 56, plates 33, 73

HABITAT AND RANGE. Mainly open country, especially farmland, but also rocky and treeless places, such as sand-dunes, and even marine islands; also occasionally in quarries and ruined buildings. Introduced in 1889–96, now resident throughout England and Wales, except the Lake District, and in Berwickshire and East Lothian in Scotland, but not yet in Ireland.

NEST. Always in a hole, usually of a tree, but also in wall, building, cliff, quarry or sand-pit, or in a burrow; exceptionally in old nest of other bird. No nest material.

EGGS AND YOUNG. *Eggs:* 3–5; almost spherical, white, somewhat glossy; incubation by hen only, 28–29 days. *Nestling:* Thick, short white down; leaves nest at about 26 days. Ring number 3.

SEASON. Late April to early July.

SONG-THRUSH *Turdus ericetorum* Plate 32 Thrush Family
PGBB, p. 57, plates 18, 21

HABITAT AND RANGE. Wherever bushes and shrubs occur, especially in gardens, town parks, hedgerows, commons, heaths, woods and copses; a common suburban bird. Resident, common throughout British Isles.

NEST. Usually in a bramble-brake, bush, hedge or low tree, but may also be 20–30 feet up in a tall tree, in creeper on a wall, or on a bank or a ledge in a shed or on a building; occasionally on the ground, but normally about 2–10 feet up. Nest rather bulky and conspicuous, though slightly smaller than blackbird's; made chiefly of dried grass and moss, and lined only with mud, fragments of rotten wood or wet dung (thus distinguishing it from blackbird's and mistle-thrush's), occasionally also with dried grass; sometimes decorated with white rags or pieces of paper, like mistle-thrush's.

EGGS AND YOUNG. *Eggs:* 3–5; blue with rather sparse black spots, sometimes zoned at big end and occasionally absent altogether; incubation by hen only, 13–14 days. *Nestling:* Longish golden-buff down, mouth golden-yellow, gape pale yellow; leaves nest at about 13 days. Ring number 1A.

SEASON. Late March to July, but February and August nests sometimes reported; two broods normal, sometimes three.

PIED WOODPECKER *Dendrocopos major* Plate 4
  PGBB, p. 57, plates 16, 23   [Woodpecker Family

HABITAT AND RANGE. All kinds of well-timbered country, broad-leaved and coniferous woods, heaths, farmland, parks and large gardens; the commonest suburban woodpecker. Resident almost throughout England and Wales; in Scotland rather local N to Great Glen and gradually spreading farther N and W; absent from Ireland.

NEST. Always in a hole in a tree, which it bores itself, usually at a height of 10 feet or more; entrance-hole slightly elliptical; no nest-material except a few wood-chips. Often dispossessed by starlings. Will use suitable nest-box.

EGGS AND YOUNG. *Eggs:* 4–7; broadly elliptical, glossy white; incubation 16 days. *Nestling:* No down; leaves nest at about 19–20 days. Ring number 2.

SEASON. Mid-May to early July.

ENTRANCE-HOLES TO NESTS OF BARRED
(*right*), PIED (*middle*) AND GREEN WOOD-
PECKERS

LAND BIRDS: Medium

GOLDEN ORIOLE *Oriolus oriolus* Plate 33 Oriole Family
PGBB, p. 58, plates 20, 21

HABITAT AND RANGE. Well-timbered parks and large gardens, especially with groves of evergreen or holm oaks. Annual spring visitor in very small numbers to S and E England, occasionally remaining to breed.

NEST. Purse-like, slung from the fork of two branches, and firmly fastened to them, not free swinging like a hammock. Made of dried grass and similar local materials, but freely decorated both inside and out with flowers, pieces of paper, etc.

EGGS AND YOUNG. *Eggs:* 3–4; white, rather sparsely marked at big end with dark purple spots; incubation 14–15 days. *Nestling:* Buffish-white down, mouth bright pink, gape whitish; leaves nest at 14–15 days. Ring number 1A.

SEASON. Late May and June.

RING-OUZEL *Turdus torquatus* Plate 13 Thrush Family
PGBB, p. 60, plates 18, 19, 23

HABITAT AND RANGE. Mountains and moorlands, especially cloughs, combes and hillsides. Summer visitor to all hilly districts N and W of a line from Humber to Lyme Regis, but distinctly local in SW England, W Wales, W Scotland, Isle of Man and Ireland.

NEST. On the ground, on a bank or in tall heather, often by a moorland stream or track; sometimes in derelict buildings or old mine-shafts, or on quarry-faces, rocky outcrops or cliffs. Made and lined mainly with dried grasses.

EGGS AND YOUNG. *Eggs:* 4; pale greenish-blue with red-brown blotches and speckles, very like a boldly marked blackbird's or mistle-thrush's; incubation 14 days. *Nestling:* Long buff down, mouth deep yellow, gape yellowish; leaves nest at 14 days. Ring number 1A.

SEASON. Mid-April to June; normally two broods.

BLACKBIRD *Turdus merula* Plate 32   Thrush Family
PGBB, p. 60, plates 18, 19, 69

HABITAT AND RANGE. Wherever bushes and shrubs occur, especially in gardens, town parks, hedgerows, heaths, woods, copses, and combes and cloughs in hills; a common suburban bird. Resident and common throughout British Isles.

NEST. Usually in a bramble brake, bush or hedge, or in such similar sites as creeper against walls or tree-trunks, tree-stumps, and stacks of pea-sticks, but quite often also in trees up to 20 or more feet from ground, and occasionally on a ledge in or on a building, or even on a bank or on the ground. Bulky and conspicuous nest, made chiefly of dried grass and often moss, lined with mud which is covered with a further lining of dried grass. Same nest sometimes used twice.

EGGS AND YOUNG. *Eggs:* 3–5; greenish-blue varying from pale to quite deep in shade, usually speckled all over with pale reddish-brown spots, but sometimes quite boldly marked; incubation by hen only, 13–14 days. *Nestling:* Long greyish down, mouth deep yellow, gape yellowish; leaves nest at 13–14 days. Ring number 1A.

SEASON. Late March to July; two broods normal, three quite common.

FIELDFARE (*Turdus pilaris*), Plate 47; Thrush Family (*PGBB*, p. 61, plates 18, 21). Has often been reported nesting in Britain, but never proved to do so, most records originating in observer's lack of familiarity with mistle-thrush. Nest like blackbird's and in rather similar situations; many eggs also like blackbird's, but others bluer and more boldly marked. A common and widespread winter visitor.

MISTLE-THRUSH *Turdus viscivorus* Plate 34
PGBB, p. 61, plate 18   [Thrush Family

HABITAT AND RANGE. Generally in cultivated country, farmland, gardens, parks, orchards, wherever there are scattered trees; also in woods, and not uncommon in suburbs. Resident and common throughout British Isles, though local in NW Scotland.

NEST. Usually 10–40 feet up in a tree, but not uncommonly lower down, and occasionally in a hedge or bush or on a ledge on a cliff or building. Bulky and conspicuous nest, made and lined mainly with dried grass over mud, but frequently decorated with white scraps of paper or rag.

EGGS AND YOUNG. *Eggs:* 3–5; pale rufous or greenish-blue, rather boldly marked with red-brown spots and blotches; incubation by hen only, 13–14 days. *Nestling:* Long buffish-white down, mouth bright yellow, gape pale yellow; leaves nest at about 15 days. Ring number 1A.

SEASON. March (sometimes February) to early June; often a second brood.

NIGHTJAR *Caprimulgus europaeus* Plate 12 Nightjar Family
PGBB, p. 62, plates 17, 29, 73

HABITAT AND RANGE. All kinds of gorsy and brackeny places, such as heaths, woodland clearings, felled woodlands, moorland cloughs and corries, and sand-dunes. Summer visitor, breeding throughout British Isles, but rather local in some districts.

NEST. A scrape on bare ground, often on border-line between tracts of bracken and heather of previous season's burning; no lining, but pieces of dead wood often nearby.

EGGS AND YOUNG. *Eggs:* 2; elliptical; various shades of whitish, marbled more or less heavily with greyish or brownish blotches; incubation 18 days. *Nestling:* Almost covered with buff and reddish-brown down; leaves nest at any time from 1 to 17 days, but often stays close by. Ring number 2 overlapped.

SEASON. Late May to August; two broods.

CORNCRAKE *Crex crex* Plate 12 Rail Family
PGBB, p. 62, plates 25, 71

HABITAT AND RANGE. Grass fields, also rough grass on hillsides and damp sedgy meadows. Summer visitor, breeding throughout Scotland and Ireland, and in N England and N and W Wales, but elsewhere either sporadically or very locally. Formerly widespread in England.

NEST. Well concealed in long grass, coarse vegetation or brambles. Roughly made of dried grass, sometimes loosely domed.

EGGS AND YOUNG. *Eggs:* 8–12; various shades of whitish, but mostly creamy, more or less heavily spotted or blotched with reddish-brown and grey; incubation mainly by hen, about 16 days. *Chick:* Covered with long, blackish-brown down; leaves nest within a few hours. Ring number 2.

SEASON. Late May to July or August; perhaps occasionally a second brood.

TURTLE-DOVE *Streptopelia turtur* Plate 32 Dove Family
PGBB, p. 63, plates 24, 29, 68

HABITAT AND RANGE. All kinds of well-timbered and bushy country, heaths, commons, open woodlands, copses, parks, large gardens. Summer visitor, common in S and E England and Midlands, local in N and SW England and in Wales. Very local in S Scotland; absent from Ireland.

NEST. Always in a tree or thick bush or hedge, from 4–8 feet, sometimes higher; occasionally on old nest of other bird. A flat, flimsy platform of slender black twigs, like a small woodpigeon's, lined with roots, etc.

EGGS AND YOUNG. *Eggs:* 2; oval or elliptical, glossy white; incubation 13–14 days. *Nestling:* Blue-grey skin with tufts of pale yellow down; leaves nest after 18 days. Ring number 2.

SEASON. Mid-May to July; two broods.

BEE-EATER (*Merops apiaster*), Plate 47; Bee-eater Family (*PGBB*, p. 63, plate 20). Two pairs bred in Sussex, 1955; unsuccessful attempts near Edinburgh, 1920. Colonial; nest-holes normally excavated in sandy bank or cliff like sand-martin; eggs round and glossy white.

HOOPOE *Upupa epops* Plate 4 Hoopoe Family
PGBB, p. 64, plates 21, 22

HABITAT AND RANGE. Parks, gardens and open country with scattered trees. Annual spring visitor in very small numbers, has occasionally bred in S England.

Nest. Always in a hole or crevice of some kind, usually in a tree, but also in walls, buildings and nest-boxes. Usually no nest material, but sometimes a few straws, feathers, etc.

Eggs and Young. *Eggs:* 5–8; broadly elliptical, greyish or yellowish, not glossy, soon stained by excrement; incubation by hen only, about 18 days. *Nestling:* Long white down, mouth bright pink, gape white; leaves nest at 20–27 days. Ring number 2.

Season. May and June.

GOLDEN PLOVER *Charadrius apricarius* Plate 13
PGBB, p. 64, plates 38, 41, 78, 82   [Plover Family

Habitat and Range. Moors, mosses and mountain tops. Summer visitor to hill country of N and W Britain and Ireland, but scarce in S Wales and only occasional in SW England. Common elsewhere in winter.

Nest. On ground, often among short heather, peat-hags or burnt vegetation. Scrape normally lined only with a few scraps of heather, but like lapwing's, occasionally well padded.

Eggs and Young. *Eggs:* 4; pear-shaped, pale to deep buff with many blackish-brown spots and blotches, generally brighter than lapwing's; incubation 27–28 days. *Chick:* Covered with golden-yellow down, mottled black; leaves nest within a few hours. Ring number 2.

Season. Mid-April to June.

MERLIN *Falco columbarius* Plates 14, 37   Falcon Family
PGBB, p. 65, plates 29, 30, 31

Habitat and Range. Moors, fells, mountains, rough hilly country, cliffs, bogs and sand-dunes. Resident, breeding rather locally throughout British Isles, except in S and E England and Midlands.

Nest. Normally on the ground, but sometimes in the old nest of a crow or other bird in a tree or on a cliff ledge. Material either lacking or very scanty, except on dunes where the hollow is fairly well lined with dried grasses.

Eggs and Young. *Eggs:* 4–5; broadly elliptical, usually

heavily suffused with reddish-brown markings, only rarely showing the whitish ground-colour; incubation about 30 days. *Nestling:* Down white or whitish at first, becoming greyish-brown; leaves nest at about 26 days. Ring number 3.
SEASON. May to mid-July.

SPARROWHAWK *Accipiter nisus* Plate 35   Hawk Family
PGBB, p. 65, plates 29, 30, 31
HABITAT AND RANGE. Woods and all kinds of well-timbered country, including the suburbs of large towns. Resident and fairly common throughout British Isles, but local in N Scotland.
NEST. Normally fairly high up in a tree, often a conifer in a deciduous wood, and usually in a main fork; exceptionally in a bush or other low site. Large, untidy nest made of twigs and sticks, sometimes lined with rotting wood or dead leaves, and occasionally built on foundation of old nest of other bird; may be used again. As with other birds of prey, the nest gradually becomes flecked with down from the growing nestlings, and occupied nests can be told in this way.
EGGS AND YOUNG. *Eggs:* 4–6; broadly elliptical, whitish, more or less heavily marked with reddish-brown spots and blotches; incubation normally by hen only, 35 days. *Nestling:* Covered with white down; leaves nest at about 27 days. Ring number 3.
SEASON. May to mid-July.

HOBBY *Falco subbuteo* Plate 35   Falcon Family
PGBB, p. 66, plates 30, 31
HABITAT AND RANGE. All kinds of country with scattered timber, especially downland with shelter-belts of pines, but also farmland, heaths and open woodland. Summer visitor, breeding locally in S England, and occasionally in Midlands as far N as Cheshire and Yorkshire.
NEST. Always well up in a tree, especially conifers. Habitually uses old nest of other bird (most often carrion-crow) or squirrel. Does not line nest, and indeed may remove lining that is already there.

Eggs and Young. *Eggs:* 3; bluntly elliptical, whitish, heavily freckled red-brown; incubation 28 days. *Nestling:* Covered with buffish-white down, later becoming greyish; leaves nest at about 30 days. Ring number 3.

Season. June and July.

LAPWING *Vanellus vanellus* Plate 16   Plover Family
PGBB, p. 67, plates 4, 45, 83

Habitat and Range. Farmland, especially arable, damp rushy grass fields, moorland and rough grassy hills, and coastal marshes. Resident and common throughout British Isles.

Nest. Tends to be social. Always on ground, sometimes in a tussock; a scrape lined with a few dried grasses, etc., but on bare arable or marshy land often a fairly substantial heap of roots and similar materials, standing a few inches above ground-level.

Eggs and Young. *Eggs:* 4; pear-shaped; olive-buff or olive-green, heavily spotted and blotched with black or blackish-brown; incubation about 27 days. *Chick:* Covered with rich brown down marbled black; leaves nest within a few hours. Ring number 2.

Season. Late March to June.

COMMON PARTRIDGE *Perdix perdix* Plate 12
PGBB, p. 68, plates 25, 26, 71   [Pheasant Family

Habitat and Range. Farmland, both grass and arable, and adjacent rough grazings, also on moors, heaths, coastal marshes, sand-dunes and tracts of shingle. Resident throughout British Isles, common over most of England and E Scotland, but scarce and local in W Scotland and most of Wales and Ireland.

Nest. Always on ground, mostly in grassy places, but also among crops, coarse vegetation and young trees, and in hedge-bottoms; exceptionally on a haystack. Scrape lined with grass, leaves, etc., and often approached by a runway.

Eggs and Young. *Eggs:* 12–17; somewhat pear-shaped, pale olive-brown; incubation by hen only, about 24 days.

Chick: Covered with buff down, liberally marked black and with chestnut patches on crown and rump; leaves nest within a few hours. Not to be ringed.

SEASON. April to June.

GREEN WOODPECKER *Picus viridis* Plate 4
PGBB, p. 68, plates 20, 21   [Woodpecker Family

HABITAT AND RANGE. All kinds of well-timbered country, from open woodlands, heaths, commons and farmland to parks and large gardens, much preferring broad-leaved to coniferous trees. Resident, common S of Humber–Mersey line, but local north of it; is gradually spreading into S Scotland though long established near Perth. Not in Ireland.

NEST. Always in a slightly elliptical hole bored in a tree, usually at a fair height from the ground; fresh nest-hole usually bored each year and chips left scattered on ground. A few chips the only lining. Often dispossessed by starlings.

EGGS AND YOUNG. *Eggs:* 5–7; oval, white, but sometimes stained brown or yellow; incubation 18–19 days. *Nestling:* No down; leaves nest at 19–20 days. Ring number 2.

SEASON. Late April to June.

CUCKOO *Cuculus canorus* Plates 11*, 30, 39 Cuckoo Family
PGBB, p. 69, plates 5, 29, 30, 31

HABITAT AND RANGE. Any type of habitat where there are small birds for it to victimise, but not the immediate seashore or cliffs, nor the centres of towns. Summer visitor, breeding almost throughout British Isles.

NEST. Invariably lays eggs in nest of another bird, usually a smaller one than itself. Chief fosterers in British Isles are meadow-pipit, hedge-sparrow, reed-warbler and pied wagtail, in approximately that order of popularity, but linnet, tree-pipit, skylark, sedge-warbler and robin are also used fairly often. Cuckoos' eggs have also been reported in the nests of some fifty other species in the British Isles.

---

* In Plate 11 the cuckoo is removing one of the pipit's eggs.

EGGS AND YOUNG. *Eggs:* Extremely variable, often approximating very closely in pattern to victim's egg, though usually larger; ground-colour can be almost any pale colour except white, with spots, blotches and speckles of some shade of brown or grey; any larger and disparate egg in a small bird's nest is most likely to be a cuckoo's; normal 'clutch' of individual hen (all laid in different nests), 12 or more; two cuckoos' eggs in one nest are likely to be product of different hens; incubation 12½ days. *Nestling:* No down, mouth brilliant deep orange, gape yellow; ejects fosterer's own eggs or young during first four days, and when fully grown may completely fill or overflow nest; leaves nest at 21–22 days. Ring number 2.

SEASON. May to July.

JACKDAW *Corvus monedula* Plate 6   Crow Family
PGBB, p. 69, plates 69, 70

HABITAT AND RANGE. Small towns, villages, cathedrals, castles, quarries, inland and sea-cliffs, farmland and parkland with old trees. Resident, common throughout British Isles, but local in N and W Scotland.

NEST. Semi-colonial. Nearly always in a hole or crevice in a building (fond of chimneys), cliff or tree, but also in burrows in a cliff-face, in the foundations of old rooks' nests and exceptionally openly in a tree. An untidy pile of fairly large sticks when space permits, especially in a hollow tree, lined with wool and other local materials.

EGGS AND YOUNG. *Eggs:* 4–6; bluish-white, usually more or less heavily marked with blackish spots and blotches, incubation by hen only, 17–18 days. *Nestling:* Shortish pale grey down, mouth purplish-pink, gape pale yellow; leaves nest at about 32 days. Ring number 3 overlapped.

SEASON. Mid-April to June.

STOCK-DOVE *Columba oenas* Plates 1, 6   Dove Family
PGBB, p. 70, plates 24, 68

HABITAT AND RANGE. Woods, parkland and farmland with old timber, inland and sea-cliffs, old buildings, sand-dunes and rabbit warrens. Resident, common throughout Great Britain, except NW Scotland; local in Ireland and Isle of Man.

NEST. Tends to be social. Usually in a hole in a tree, building, cliff or sand-pit, but also in rabbit-burrows, nest-boxes, and hollows in trees, especially pollards; exceptionally openly in hedges, and on ground. Little or no nest material when in holes, otherwise uses twigs like woodpigeon.

EGGS AND YOUNG. *Eggs:* 2; broadly elliptical, glossy white; incubation about 17 days. *Nestling:* Rather sparse yellow down, mouth pink, gape pale flesh; leaves nest at about 27 days. Ring number 3, overlapped; young not to be ringed till well feathered.

SEASON. Late March to early October; two broods, often three.

LONDON PIGEON *Columba livia* Plate 40 Dove Family *PGBB*, p. 113, plates 24, 68

HABITAT AND RANGE. All large and many small cities and towns, especially ports, also in quarries and on coastal cliffs in England and Wales (in some places still with a large admixture of genuine wild rock-dove stock).

NEST. Colonial; always on a ledge on or in a hole in a building; ledges under bridges a favourite site. Scantily made of twigs, coarse grasses and other local materials.

EGGS AND YOUNG. Presumably all as Rock-Dove (p. 96), but little separate information.

SEASON. March to September; probably at least two broods.

EASTERN COLLARED DOVE (*Streptopelia decaocto*), Plate 47; Dove Family (*PGBB*, *p.* 59). Has spread rapidly over Europe from the Balkans in recent years, and since 1955 a good many pairs have been breeding regularly in Britain, as far north as Morayshire. Nests and eggs intermediate between woodpigeon and turtle-dove, but prefers breeding in high trees, especially cedars, also planes or sycamores.

KESTREL *Falco tinnunculus* Plates 37, 40   Falcon Family
PGBB, p. 70, plates 29, 31

HABITAT AND RANGE. All types of country from the centres of
large cities to wild and remote coastal and mountain districts; not uncommon in suburbs. Resident throughout
British Isles, and the commonest British bird of prey.

NEST. On a ledge of a cliff or high building, or on the old nest
of another bird (most often carrion-crow or magpie), occasionally in a hollow tree or even on the ground. No nest
material, but old nests of other birds are flattened out.

EGGS AND YOUNG. *Eggs:* 4–5; bluntly elliptical, either white
heavily freckled with reddish-brown, or wholly suffused with
reddish-brown; incubation about 28 days. *Nestling:* Covered
with short white down, later turning buffish-grey; leaves nest
at 28–29 days. Ring number 3.

SEASON. Mid-April to July.

JAY *Garrulus glandarius* Plate 34   Crow Family
PGBB, p. 71, plates 21, 22

HABITAT AND RANGE. Woods, copses and well-timbered heaths
and commons; sometimes in town parks and large gardens.
Resident and common in England and Wales, but local in
Scotland and Ireland.

NEST. Almost always in a bush, hedge or small tree, usually
6–20 feet up but occasionally much higher; sometimes among
epicormic shoots on a tree-trunk, or in tangle of honeysuckle
or old man's beard near tree-bole. Made of sticks and twigs,
and lined with black rootlets and hair.

EGGS AND YOUNG. *Eggs:* 5–6; like a large, finely freckled
blackbird's, green thickly speckled with olive-brown, and
often with a black hairstreak; incubation by hen only, about
16 days. *Nestling:* No down, mouth pale pink, gape pinkish;
leaves nest at about 20 days. Ring number 3 overlapped.

SEASON. Late April to June.

PALLAS'S SAND-GROUSE (*Syrrhaptes paradoxus*), Plate 45;
Sand-grouse Family. Sporadic visitor irrupting at intervals
(none since 1909), staying to breed in Yorks in 1888 and

Morayshire in 1888–89 following great invasion of 1888. Buffish eggs with purplish-brown markings are normally laid in scrape on ground in sandy places.

BARN-OWL *Tyto alba* Plates 6, 40 Owl Family
PGBB, p. 72, plates 33, 74, 76

HABITAT AND RANGE. Farmland, especially near villages, also cliffs and rough open country. Resident throughout British Isles, but scarce and local in N. Scotland.

NEST. In ruins, barns, church towers, hollow trees, cliffs, quarries, ricks or decaying thatch. Eggs laid on floor or ledge or in crevice with no material except old castings, which may have accumulated over an occupation of many years. Will use nest-boxes.

EGGS AND YOUNG. *Eggs:* 4–6; elliptical and not so blunt as tawny owl's, matt white; incubation by hen only but often accompanied by cock, about 33 days. *Nestling:* Almost covered with short white down; leaves nest at 9–12 weeks. Ring number 4.

SEASON. Almost throughout the year, but most often from late April to June; a second brood not infrequent, and may be laid beside still unfledged young.

LONG-EARED OWL *Asio otus* Plates 14, 34 Owl Family
PGBB, p. 72, plates 33, 73

HABITAT AND RANGE. Woods, especially coniferous; less often heaths, thickets, marshes and sand-dunes. Resident throughout British Isles, but local in S England and Midlands and very local in Wales and NW Scotland.

NEST. Usually in trees in old nests of other birds (most often crows and magpies) or squirrels, but not infrequently on bare ground among undergrowth in woods or on heaths or dunes.

EGGS AND YOUNG. *Eggs:* 4–5; elliptical, white, rather glossy; incubation mainly by hen, 27–28 days. *Nestling:* Covered with short white down; leaves nest at 23–24 days. Ring number 4.

SEASON. March (occasionally February) to early June.

WOODCOCK   *Scolopax rusticola*   Plate 12
PGBB, p. 73, plates 25, 39, 73   [Sandpiper Family

HABITAT AND RANGE. Woodland and rough ground with shrubs or other cover. Resident; common in the Weald, the New Forest, the Welsh Marches, N Midlands, N England, and many parts of Scotland and Ireland; scarce and local elsewhere, most often in Wales, SW England, and coastal strip from N. Norfolk to Thames estuary.

NEST. Always in a scrape on the ground, often close to a tree, but also in the open or under cover of vegetation, such as brambles or bracken. Lined with dead leaves.

EGGS AND YOUNG. *Eggs:* 4; one end bluntly pointed, but not pear-shaped like most waders; various shades of greyish-white, buff and brown, with reddish-brown and greyish blotches usually fairly thick; incubation by hen only, about 21 days. *Chick:* Covered with buff down marbled chestnut; leaves nest within a few hours. Ring number 2.

SEASON. Mid-March to June; often two broods.

PTARMIGAN   *Lagopus mutus*   Plate 15   Grouse Family
PGBB, p. 73, plate 26

HABITAT AND RANGE. Barren, stony mountain-tops, usually above 2,500 feet. Resident, confined to the highest Scottish mountains from Ben Lomond northwards, and in some Inner Hebrides.

NEST. Always in a scrape on the ground, sometimes among sparse vegetation or under a rock. Austerely lined with scraps of dry grass and other local materials.

EGGS AND YOUNG. *Eggs:* 5–9; similar to red grouse (below), but smaller and often with paler ground-colour; incubation by hen only, about 25 days. *Chick:* Covered with buff down, marbled black; paler than red grouse; leaves nest within a few hours. Not to be ringed.

SEASON. Mid-May to early July.

RED GROUSE   *Lagopus scoticus*   Plate 15   Grouse Family
PGBB, p. 74, plates 26, 71

HABITAT AND RANGE. Moors, mosses and bogs, with heather

or crowberry (rarely grass). Resident, common on all suitable moorlands in Scotland, England S to Cannock Chase (also introduced on Exmoor) and Wales (not Glamorgan or Pembroke); scarce in Ireland.

NEST. Always a scrape on the ground or in a tussock, usually among vegetation. Sparsely lined with dried grass and various other local materials.

EGGS AND YOUNG. *Eggs:* 6–11; Buffish or reddish-brown, heavily blotched and speckled darker red-brown; incubation by hen only, 24–25 days. *Chick:* Covered with buff down marbled chestnut and black, can be told from black grouse by down on toes; leaves nest within a few hours. Not to be ringed.

SEASON. April to June.

RED-LEGGED PARTRIDGE *Alectoris rufa* Plate 12
PGBB, p. 74, plates 25, 26, 71   [Pheasant Family

HABITAT AND RANGE. Cultivated farmland, especially arable, also stony and sandy heaths and wastes, extensive shingle tracts and downland. Resident (introduced), common in E and SE England, gradually thinning out through the Midlands N to Yorkshire and N Wales and W to Somerset.

NEST. Normally in a scrape in the ground under cover or in a hedge-bottom, but occasionally on or in side of a stack. Sparsely lined with dried grass and other local materials.

EGGS AND YOUNG. *Eggs:* 9–16; much larger and less pear-shaped than common partridge's, and quite distinctly coloured, being pale buffish well sprinkled with reddish-brown spots and blotches; incubation 23–24 days. *Chick:* Covered with buff down, marbled chestnut; leaves nest within a few hours. Not to be ringed.

SEASON. Late April to June.

SHORT-EARED OWL *Asio flammeus* Plate 14
PGBB, p. 75, plates 33, 74   [Owl Family

HABITAT AND RANGE. Resident; local in Scotland, N England, E Anglia and W Wales, sporadic elsewhere in England and Wales, depending on the abundance of field-voles (its main food). All kinds of open country favoured by field-voles, moors, downs, rough hillsides, heaths, bogs, fens, marshes, sand-dunes and very young plantations.

NEST. Always in a scrape on the ground under cover of rushes or other vegetation. Scantily lined with dried grass and other local materials.

EGGS AND YOUNG. *Eggs:* 4–7; almost spherical, white, rather glossy; incubation by hen only, about 26 days. *Nestling:* Covered with pale buff down; young scatter among surrounding vegetation after about 14–15 days. Ring number 4.

SEASON. April to June or July; two broods when supply of voles plentiful.

COMMON AND RED-LEGGED PARTRIDGES
(EGG AND CHICK)

LAND BIRDS: Medium Long

TAWNY OWL *Strix aluco* Plate 4   Owl Family
PGBB, p. 75, plates 33, 73

HABITAT AND RANGE. Woods, copses and well-timbered parks, gardens and farmland; not uncommon in suburbs. Resident, common throughout most of Great Britain, but absent from Ireland and Isle of Man.

NEST. Normally in a hole or deep fork of a tree, but sometimes in old nest of crow or other bird, or squirrel's drey, on ledge of cliff or building, or even on ground under cover, in angle of tree-roots, or in burrow; will use suitable nest-box. No nest material.

EGGS AND YOUNG. *Eggs:* 2–4; almost spherical, matt white; incubation by hen only, about 29 days. *Nestling:* Covered with white down; leaves nest at about 35 days. Ring number 4.

SEASON. Mid-March (exceptionally February) to mid-June.

CHOUGH *Coracia pyrrhocorax* Plates 8, 9   Crow Family
PGBB, p. 76, plates 23, 69, 70

HABITAT AND RANGE. Cliff-bound sea-coasts, and hilly districts with quarries or old mine-shafts. Resident, fairly common on N, W and S coasts Ireland and Isle of Man; local on coasts N Cornwall, SW and NW Wales, and Inner Hebrides, also inland in N and C Wales and in Ireland.

NEST. Tends to be social. Always in a crevice or hole in a cliff, sea-cave, quarry-face or old mine-shaft. An untidy crow-like pile of sticks and other local materials, well lined with wool and hair.

EGGS AND YOUNG. *Eggs:* 4–6; white, tinted cream or green, with spots and blotches of various shades of greyish-brown; incubation by hen only, 17–18 days. *Nestling:* Down short, sparse and grey-brown; mouth pink with white spurs on

palate, gape yellow; leaves nest at about 38 days. Ring
number 3 overlapped.

SEASON. April to June.

PEREGRINE *Falco peregrinus* Plate 38   Falcon Family
PGBB, p. 76, plates 29, 30, 31

HABITAT AND RANGE. Resident, breeding on all cliff-bound
coasts and hilly districts in British Isles, but very scarce
inland S and E of line from Humber to Severn and thence to
Lyme Regis.

NEST. Almost always on a ledge or in a cavity in a cliff, very
exceptionally on a tall building, or on ground on marine
island. No nest material, but will use old nest of raven or
other large bird.

EGGS AND YOUNG. *Eggs:* 3–4; bluntly elliptical, red-brown
(sometimes with white showing through), heavily suffused
with darker red-brown markings; incubation 28–29 days.
Nestling: Covered with whitish down, becoming buffer;
leaves nest at about 38 days. Ring number Clip 4.

SEASON. April to early July.

STONE-CURLEW *Burhinus oedicnemus* Plate 13
PGBB, p. 77, plates 25, 73   [Stone-curlew Family

HABITAT AND RANGE. Sandy heaths and warrens, open stony
fields, chalk downland and extensive tracts of shingle.
Summer visitor, rather local, now only on the brecklands and
coastal heaths of E Anglia, at Dungeness, locally on the
Chilterns and South Downs, and in a good many places on
the main mass of the Wessex chalklands.

NEST. Almost invariably in a scrape on the bare ground, but exceptionally among vegetation. No lining, but eggs often laid
on or close to white stones, rabbit pellets or other small objects.

EGGS AND YOUNG. *Eggs:* 2; both shape and size variable;
bluntly elliptical to ovate; buffish, usually rather heavily
marked with dark brown blotches; incubation about 26 days.
Chick: Covered with buff down, streaked with black lines;
leaves nest within a few hours. Ring number 3.

SEASON. Mid-April to August; two broods occasionally.

WOODPIGEON *Columba palumbus* Plate 34 Dove Family
PGBB, p. 77, plates 24, 68

HABITAT AND RANGE. All kinds of wooded country; regular in town parks and large gardens. Resident, common almost everywhere, but local in N Scotland.

NEST. Normally in a tree, especially a conifer, or among ivy on a tree, but also sometimes in quite low bushes and occasionally on the ground among heather, exceptionally on a building; most nests between 5 and 15 feet, but sometimes 40 feet or more. Nest normally a platform of thin black twigs, through which the eggs show when first laid, but this is often lined with roots, etc., and is strengthened when the young hatch.

EGGS AND YOUNG. *Eggs:* 2; white, almost elliptical, slightly glossy; incubation 17–18 days. *Nestling:* Scantily covered with tufts of yellowish hairy down; mouth pink, gape pale flesh; leaves nest at 33–34 days. Ring number 3.

SEASON. Late March to September, but nests may occasionally be found in any month; two broods normal, perhaps sometimes three.

BLACK GROUSE *Lyrurus tetrix* Plate 15 Grouse Family
PGBB, p. 78, plates 26–28, 72

HABITAT AND RANGE. Moorland with scattered trees, especially birches, and on the borders of moorland and woodland. Resident, local and decreasing almost everywhere; Exmoor, C and N Wales, the Pennines N from Staffordshire, Scotland.

NEST. Normally in a scrape in the ground under cover, especially among rushes in dampish site; exceptionally in old nest of other bird in a tree.

EGGS AND YOUNG. *Eggs:* 6–10; buffish, rather sparsely spotted various shades of reddish-brown; incubation by hen only, about 27 days. *Chick:* Buff marbled black; leaves nest within a few hours. Not to be ringed.

SEASON. May and June.

MONTAGU'S HARRIER *Circus pygargus* Plate 17
PGBB, p. 79, plates 32, 74, 76 [Hawk Family

HABITAT AND RANGE. Open and usually rough country, including heaths, downs, moors, dunes, salt and fresh marshes, reed-beds, fens, young plantations, and occasionally even cornfields. Summer visitor, very local in most coastal counties from Norfolk southwards and round to Anglesey, more rarely inland and in N England.

NEST. Tends to be social. Always on ground under cover of vegetation. Made of sedges and other local materials.

EGGS AND YOUNG. *Eggs:* 4; broadly elliptical, white or pale bluish; incubation by hen only, 28–29 days. *Nestling:* Covered with white down, becoming buffish; fledging 33–34 days, but at varying times before this the young often scatter from the nest and go into hiding in thick cover. Ring number 3.

SEASON. Late May to July.

HEN-HARRIER *Circus cyaneus* Plate 14   Hawk Family
PGBB, p. 79, plates 32, 74, 76

HABITAT AND RANGE. Moorlands. Resident in Orkney, and very locally in Scottish Highlands and Outer Hebrides; has exceptionally bred in England and Wales, but almost all alleged hen-harriers breeding south of the Border turn out to be Montagu's. Widespread as winter visitor.

NEST. Always in a scrape on the ground, built of dried grasses and various other local materials.

EGGS AND YOUNG. *Eggs:* 4–5; slightly larger than Montagu's, ground-colour bluish-white, very occasionally speckled with reddish-brown; incubation by hen only, 36–37 days. *Nestling:* Hardly distinguishable from Montagu's; leaves nest at about 5–6 weeks. Ring number 3.

SEASON. Mid-May to early July.

GREAT BLACK WOODPECKER (*Dryocopus martius*), Plate
47; Woodpecker Family (*PGBB*, p. 80, plate 23). Nest in hole in tree; eggs white. Said to have bred in Surrey for three years running in 1840's and more plausibly in Hampshire in 1862, but neither record can now be validated.

MAGPIE *Pica pica* Plate 34   Crow Family
PGBB, p. 81, plates 23, 70

HABITAT AND RANGE. Open country with trees, or at least substantial bushes; sometimes in suburbs. Resident, common in England and Wales, local in Scotland and Ireland.

NEST. A unique structure, the only large domed nest of a British bird. Always in a tree, hedge or bush, from 4–40 feet from ground. Nest and dome both made of sticks and twigs, often thorny, lined with mud covered by rootlets.

EGGS AND YOUNG. *Eggs:* 5–8; various shades of pale green, heavily sprinkled with grey-brown spots and speckles; incubation by hen only, 17–18 days. *Nestling:* No down, mouth pink inside with white spurs at base of tongue and palate; gape pale pink; leaves nest at 24–25 days. Ring number 3 overlapped.

SEASON. Nest-building begins late March, eggs in April and May, young in May and June.

CARRION-CROW   ROOK   MAGPIE

ROOK *Corvus frugilegus* Plate 34   Crow Family
PGBB, p. 81, plates 69, 70

HABITAT AND RANGE. Mainly farmland, but also in suburbs and small towns. Resident and common, but local in N and W Scotland.

NEST. Normally highly colonial, but occasionally nests singly or in very small groups. Rookeries are most often in a clump of trees near a farm or village, but also in isolated clumps, small (and sometimes even large) woods, suburbs, and the centres of towns as large as Bristol. Normally 30 or more feet up in the branches of a tree, but occasionally in small trees, bushes, or even on electric pylons and buildings. Nest a substantial pile of sticks held together with mud, often built on last year's old nest (which may also be repaired); lined with dried grass and other local materials.

EGGS AND YOUNG. *Eggs:* 5; various shades of pale green, from greyish to bluish, heavily mottled with dark greyish-brown; incubation by hen only, about 17 days. *Nestling:* Sparse dark grey down, mouth pink, gape pale yellowish-flesh; leaves nest at 29–30 days. Ring number 3.

SEASON. Nest-building begins March, eggs in late March and April, young usually leave nest in mid-May.

CARRION-CROW *Corvus corone* Plates 37, 40
PGBB, p. 81, plates 69, 70   [Crow Family

HABITAT AND RANGE. Almost universal, including sea-cliffs, town parks and suburbs. Resident and common in England, Wales and S Scotland; interbreeds with hooded crow in a narrow band from Galloway to Morayshire; absent from Isle of Man, has bred in Ireland.

NEST. Usually 30–40 feet up in a tree, but sometimes lower and even in bushes in treeless districts; also quite commonly on ledges of cliffs, especially on the coast; exceptionally on buildings. Nest similar to rook's, but when in trees can be told from occasional solitary rooks' nests by flatter appearance, and tendency to build in a stout fork rather than up in the swaying branches.

EGGS AND YOUNG. *Eggs:* 4–5; similar to rook's, but larger and ground-colour is more often blue-green; incubation by hen only, 19–20 days. *Nestling:* Similar to rook, but down more plentiful; leaves nest at about 33 days. Ring number 3.

SEASON. Last days of March to May and June.

HOODED CROW *Corvus cornix* Plates 14, 37
PGBB, p. 82, plates 69, 70   [Crow Family

HABITAT AND RANGE. Mountainous or hilly country and sea-cliffs for the most part, but within its range almost as universal as the carrion-crow. Resident in Ireland, Isle of Man, and N and W Scotland, where it overlaps and inter-breeds with the carrion-crow; elsewhere a winter visitor only.

NEST. Similar to carrion-crow, but not uncommonly on ground among heather in some districts, and not recorded on buildings.

EGGS AND YOUNG. *Eggs:* 4–6; similar to carrion-crow's; incubation by hen only, 19 days. *Nestling:* Hardly distin-guishable from carrion-crow; leaves nest at about 32 days. Ring number 3.

SEASON. Late March to May and June.

GOSHAWK (*Accipiter gentilis*), Plate 35; Hawk Family (*PGBB*, p. 82, plate 75). Normally makes a bulky sparrow-hawk-like nest of sticks fairly high up in a tree, or adapts old nest of other large bird. Eggs white or bluish-white. Has bred several times in recent years in Sussex (probably escaped falconry birds), and also exceptionally elsewhere.

COMMON BUZZARD *Buteo buteo* Plate 38 Hawk Family
PGBB, p. 82, plates 34, 75

HABITAT AND RANGE. Hilly and mountainous districts, sea-cliffs and marine islands, and in S also woods and wooded valleys and combes. Resident, common in SW England, Wales and parts of N England, more local in S and SE England, Cotswolds, Welsh Marches and Scotland; absent from E Anglia, Midlands, Ireland and Isle of Man. An increasing species.

NEST. Usually fairly high up in a tree or on a cliff-ledge, but in some districts not infrequently on the ground. A bulky nest of sticks, based sometimes on an old nest of another bird, lined with various local materials, and habitually decorated with leafy boughs, or on the coast seaweed, which are changed when they wither.

EGGS AND YOUNG. *Eggs:* 3; broadly elliptical to almost spherical, white often heavily blotched reddish-brown, but sometimes only spotted; incubation about 28 days. *Nestling:* Covered with greyish down; leaves nest at about 6–7 weeks. Ring number clip 4.

SEASON. Mid-April to July.

HONEY-BUZZARD (*Pernis apivorus*); Plate 35; Hawk Family (*PGBB*, p. 84, plates 34, 75). Nest similar to common buzzard, including green decorations, but always well up in a tree in a large wood, and often on foundation of old nest of other bird. Eggs usually much more heavily marked and often completely suffused red-brown. Now breeds only at long intervals in the larger woodlands of Midlands and S England, especially New Forest.

'WITCHES' BROOMS' (OFTEN MISTAKEN FOR BIRDS' NESTS)

LAND BIRDS: Long

PHEASANT *Phasianus colchicus* Plate 17 Pheasant Family
PGBB, p. 85, plates 25, 27, 28, 71, 72

HABITAT AND RANGE. All kinds of woodland and farmland interspersed with woods and copses, also well-timbered heaths and commons, reed- and sedge-beds, and even large gardens. Resident (introduced), common throughout most of Great Britain, but scarce in parts of Scotland and Wales, and in Ireland.

NEST. Almost always in a scrape in the ground well hidden by undergrowth; very exceptionally on a stack or similar artificial erection, or even up in a tree in an old nest or drey. Scantily lined with dried grass and other local materials.

EGGS AND YOUNG. *Eggs:* 8–15; pale olive-brown; incubation by hen only, 24–25 days. *Chick:* Covered with buff down marbled black and chestnut; leaves nest within a few hours. Not to be ringed.

SEASON. Mid-April to May; normally one brood only, but very exceptionally also in autumn.

N.B.—Several other species of pheasant have been introduced from time to time, and their nests may be found in similar positions to the common pheasant, viz. Silver Pheasant (*PGBB*, p. 84, plates 27, 28), Japanese Pheasant (*PGBB*, p. 86), Golden Pheasant (*PGBB*, p. 86, plates 27, 28), Lady Amherst's Pheasant (*PGBB*, p. 86, plates 27, 28), and Reeves's Pheasant (*PGBB*, p. 89, plates 27, 28).

CAPERCAILLIE *Tetrao urogallus* Plate 15 Grouse Family
PGBB, p. 86, plates 27, 28, 72

HABITAT AND RANGE. Pine and other coniferous woods, occasionally on open moors. Resident (reintroduced) throughout central Scottish Highlands, S to Stirlingshire and N to SE Sutherland, also locally or sporadically in Argyll and Tweed valley.

NEST. Almost always in a scrape on ground among vegetation,

often at foot of a tree; exceptionally in an old nest in a tree. Lined with various local materials; eggs covered with pine needles before incubation begins.

EGGS AND YOUNG. *Eggs:* 5–8; buff well sprinkled with brownish spots; incubation by hen only, about 28 days. *Chick:* Covered with buff down marbled chestnut and black; leaves nest within a few hours. Not to be ringed.

SEASON. Late April to early June.

KITE *Milvus milvus* Plate 35　　　　　　Hawk Family
　PGBB, p. 87, plates 34, 75

HABITAT AND RANGE. Wooded valleys in Central Wales; very local.

NEST. Always well up in a tree in a wood. A bulky affair of sticks bound together with mud and lined with a heterogeneous collection of local materials, including often rags, bits of paper, etc. ('When the kite builds, look to lesser linen'—*A Winter's Tale*.)

EGGS AND YOUNG. *Eggs:* 2–3; similar to buzzard's, but often only faintly marked; incubation by hen only, about 29 days. *Nestling:* Covered with down of various shades of buff; leaves nest at about 7–8 weeks. Ring number Clip 4, but Welsh kites are very shy and desert easily, so the temptation to look for or visit nests at any time before fledging should be resisted.

SEASON. Mid-April to July.

RAVEN *Corvus corax* Plate 38　　　　　　Crow Family
　PGBB, p. 87, plates 69, 70

HABITAT AND RANGE. Hilly and mountainous country, and sea-cliffs. Resident in most coastal counties except between Moray and I.O.W., and in most inland counties E of a line from Portland Bill to the mouth of the Tyne; quite common in some western coastal areas.

NEST. Usually on a ledge of a sea-cliff, inland cliff or crag, or quarry-face, but in some districts not uncommonly in trees; occasionally on a steep declivity but not on flat ground. A substantial pile of sticks and other local materials, bound together with mud and lined with hair, wool, etc.

EGGS AND YOUNG. *Eggs:* 4–6; like hooded and carrion-crows' but larger; incubation by hen only, 20–21 days. *Nestling:* Short brownish down, mouth purplish pink, gape yellowish flesh; leaves nest at about 5–6 weeks. Ring number Clip 4.

SEASON. February to April and May.

YOUNG RAVEN

LAND BIRDS: Very Long

GOLDEN EAGLE *Aquila chrysaëtus* Plate 38 Hawk Family
PGBB, p. 88, plates 34, 77

HABITAT AND RANGE. Mountainous country in the Scottish
Highlands and Hebrides, also very locally in Galloway.

NEST. Usually on a ledge of an inland crag or cliff, but in some
districts quite commonly in isolated trees, and in a few places
also on sea-cliffs, or even on the ground. An immense pile
of sticks, lined with various local materials, including heather
and other fresh greenery.

EGGS AND YOUNG. *Eggs:* 2; bluntly elliptical, white more or
less heavily marked red-brown (eggs in same clutch often
dissimilar, one being almost unmarked); incubation mainly
by hen, about 40 days. *Nestling:* Covered with whitish
down; leaves nest at about 12–13 weeks. Ring size M.

SEASON. Mid-March to mid-July.

GREAT BUSTARD (*Otis tarda*), Plate 46; Bustard Family
(*PGBB*, p. 89). Large olive eggs with brownish markings laid
always on ground in open country or farmland, but has not
bred in Britain since 1832.

79

LAND BIRDS: Huge

WHITE STORK (*Ciconia ciconia*), Plate 46; Stork Family
(*PGBB*, p. 89, plates 45, 86). Huge nest of sticks on buildings,
artificial nest-sites on poles or pedestals, or in trees, eggs
white. Has bred in Britain only once, on St. Giles's Cathe-
dral, Edinburgh, in 1416, according to the old chronicler
Abbot Bower.

WHITE STORK AND NEST

WATERSIDE BIRDS: Very Short

SAND-MARTIN *Riparia riparia* Plates 8, 9 Swallow **Family**
PGBB, p. 90, plates 9, 65

HABITAT AND RANGE. Open country, lakes and rivers. Summer visitor, common over most of British Isles, but scarce and local in N Scotland and in chalk and limestone districts of S and E England.

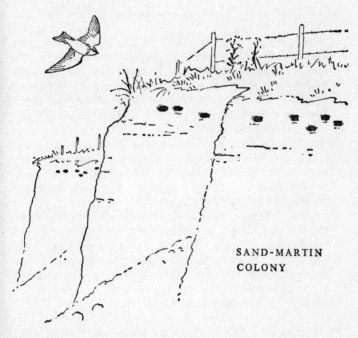

SAND-MARTIN
COLONY

NEST. Colonial. Always in a hole, usually excavated in a natural or artificial bank or low cliff, such as a river-bank, low sea-cliff, sand- or gravel-pit or railway cutting; occasionally in high sand-dunes, or in artificial holes, such as drain-pipes or weep-holes in brick embankments. Lining of dried grasses, feathers and other materials caught in the air.

EGGS AND YOUNG. *Eggs:* 4–5; matt white; incubation about 14 days. *Nestling:* Short pale grey down, mouth pale yellow, gape pale yellow; leaves nest at about 19 days. Not to be ringed as nestling.

SEASON. Excavation begins early April, nest-building in mid-April, first eggs in late April, but most from mid-May; normally two broods, with young in nest till August or early September.

REED-WARBLER *Acrocephalus scirpaceus* Plate 30
PGBB, p. 90, plate 3   [Warbler Family

HABITAT AND RANGE. Reed-beds by lakes, ponds and rivers, also occasionally osier-beds and other areas of coarse vegetation near water; exceptionally among elders, lilacs or other bushes away from water. Summer visitor, fairly common S and E of a line from the Humber to the Mersey and thence S to Lyme Regis; local in N and SW England and S Wales; absent from Scotland and Ireland.

NEST. Colonial; the great majority of nests are attached to stems of the common reed *Phragmites communis*; also occasionally to osiers and other bushes and coarse vegetation. Nest a neat, deep cup of dried grasses, lined with various local materials.

EGGS AND YOUNG. *Eggs:* 4–5; greenish-white fairly heavily marked with olive-grey specks, spots and blotches; incubation 12 days. *Nestling:* No down, mouth orange-yellow with two oval black spots at base of tongue, gape pale yellow; leaves nest at 10–11 days. Ring number 1 overlapped. One of the commonest victims of the cuckoo.

SEASON. May to August; two broods quite frequent.

MOUSTACHED WARBLER (*Lusciniola melanopogon*), Plate 43. Warbler Family. Bred in Cambridgeshire, 1946. Closely resembles sedge-warbler, but has darker cap, whiter eye-stripe and throat, and quite different song. Nest always over fresh water, eggs closely resemble sedge-warbler's.

MARSH-WARBLER *Acrocephalus palustris* Plate 30
    PGBB, p. 91, plate 3   [Warbler Family
HABITAT AND RANGE. Lush and coarse vegetation growing up
among smallish groups of trees, such as osier-beds, small
riverside copses and other places overgrown with meadow-
sweet and willow-herb; also often away from water in bean-
and cornfields, orchards, dry gravel-pits, etc. Very local
summer visitor, regular only in parts of S England (Dorset,
Somerset and valleys of lower Severn, Stratford Avon and
upper Thames), but has bred sporadically in several other
S and midland counties.
NEST. Social. Always in nettles or other thick vegetation and
often near water; normally fairly low down, but occasionally
a few feet up in a bush. Nest much less deep than reed-
warbler's and more like common whitethroat's, can be told
from all other warbler nests except blackcap's by being
fastened to adjacent stems of stout plants by so-called
'basket-handles'. Made of dried grasses, etc. and lined with
various local materials.
EGGS AND YOUNG. *Eggs:* 4–5; tend to be more sparsely and
boldly blotched than reed-warbler's and can have bluish as
well as greenish ground-colour; incubation 12 days. *Nestling:*
No down, mouth bright canary yellow with similar tongue-
spots to reed-warbler, gape yellowish-white; leaves nest at
about 12 days. Ring number 1 overlapped. Not infrequently
victimised by cuckoo.
SEASON. Last few days of May to mid-July.

SEDGE-WARBLER *Acrocephalus schoenobaenus* Plate 30
    PGBB, p. 91, plate 3   [Warbler Family
HABITAT AND RANGE. Places where coarse, rank vegetation
grows up over bushes and hedges, usually fairly near water,
e.g. fens, osier- and reed-beds, the margins of lakes, ponds,
rivers and streams, bramble-brakes on marshy ground.
Summer visitor, common almost throughout British Isles.
NEST. Social. Low down in nettles, brambles, sedges, etc., or
in a hedge or bush, usually close to fresh water, rarely above
4 feet. Nest more solid and substantially built, and markedly

shallower than reed-warbler's, and usually not actually attached to vegetation; made of dried grasses, etc., lined with various materials.

EGGS AND YOUNG. *Eggs:* 5–6; yellowish-green or yellowish-brown, heavily sprinkled with grey-brown speckles; incubation 12–13 days. *Nestling:* No down, but has greasy, oily appearance; mouth orange-yellow with a long black spot on each tongue-spur, gape pale yellow; leaves nest at 13–14 days. Ring number 1 overlapped. Often victimised by cuckoo.

SEASON. Mid-May to June or July; two broods occasional.

SAVI'S WARBLER (*Locustella luscinioides*), Plate 43; Warbler Family. Formerly bred in the Fens, but not since 1856. Closely resembles grasshopper-warbler, but has no spots on plumage. Nest among dead reeds and sedge, of dried blades of reed-grass. Eggs white, freckled grey-brown.

LITTLE RINGED PLOVER CHICK

WATERSIDE BIRDS: Short

TEMMINCK'S STINT (*Calidris temminckii*), Plate 21; Sandpiper Family (*PGBB*, p. 93, plates 37, 79). Has bred unsuccessfully twice in Inverness-shire (1934, 1936) and once in Yorkshire (1951). Four pear-shaped eggs, greenish or buffish spotted brown, laid in scrape on ground near fresh water.

REED-BUNTING *Emberiza schoeniclus* Plate 30
PGBB, p. 94, plates 13, 15 [Finch Family
HABITAT AND RANGE. Almost any kind of marshy place, fens, reed-beds, rushy fields, river banks, lakesides, osier-beds, etc. Resident, common throughout British Isles.
NEST. Nearly always low down (rarely above 1 foot) in thick vegetation, often actually on ground or in a tussock of grass; made of dried grass, lined with various local materials.
EGGS AND YOUNG. *Eggs:* 4–5; olive-brown, stone-coloured or greenish-white, more boldly marked with blackish spots and scrawls than other native buntings; incubation mainly by hen, 13–14 days. *Nestling:* Longish black down, mouth cerise with whitish spurs and tip of tongue, gape yellowish-white; leaves nest at 11–12 days. Ring number 1 overlapped.
SEASON. Late April to June or July; two broods, occasionally three.

LITTLE RINGED PLOVER *Charadrius dubius* Plate 21
PGBB, p. 94, plates 38, 79 [Plover Family
HABITAT AND RANGE. Gravel-pits, sewage farms, river shoals, and other places with extensive areas of sand, gravel or shingle near fresh water. Summer visitor; first known to have bred, 1938; has nested regularly since 1944 in SE England, mainly in valleys of Thames below Goring gap, Lea and Colne, and since 1948 in Yorkshire; also in a few other counties, e.g. Derbyshire, Gloucestershire, Northants, Suffolk.
NEST. Always a scrape on the ground, usually on gravel or shingle, but sometimes on grassy or arable land. Occasionally

lined with odd scraps of local materials; sometimes containing a few small pebbles.

EGGS AND YOUNG. *Eggs:* 4; general appearance like ringed plover's, but spotting smaller and browner; size smaller than either ringed or Kentish plover's and more pear-shaped than latter's; incubation about 25 days. *Chick:* Similar to ringed plover; leaves nest within a few hours. Ring number 1A.

SEASON. Late April to July; perhaps sometimes two broods.

KENTISH PLOVER *Charadrius alexandrinus* Plate 25
PGBB, p. 95, plates 38, 79   [Plover Family

HABITAT AND RANGE. Extensive shingle banks. Summer visitor; still occasionally breeds in SW Kent and SE Sussex, and perhaps very locally elsewhere on E and SE coasts England.

NEST. Always in a scrape on dried mud or bare shingle, sometimes lined with seaweed and other local materials.

EGGS AND YOUNG. *Eggs:* 3; pale buff well sprinkled with black spots, smaller and much less pear-shaped than ringed plover's; incubation 24 days. *Chick:* Like ringed plover, but paler; leaves nest within a few hours. Ring number 1A.

SEASON. Early May to June and July; perhaps sometimes two broods.

ROCK-PIPIT *Anthus spinoletta* Plates 2, 9, 25
PGBB, p. 95, plates 8, 37   [Wagtail Family

HABITAT AND RANGE. Rocky sea-coasts. Resident, common on all W and N coasts Great Britain and Ireland, more local on S and E coasts. In Outer Hebrides also on moorland.

NEST. Normally in a hole in a cliff, but sometimes in bank, ground or wall; occasionally concealed in vegetation. Nest of dried grass, lined with local materials.

EGGS AND YOUNG. *Eggs:* 4–5; greyish-white, thickly speckled and spotted grey-brown, larger than meadow-pipit's; incubation by hen only, about 14 days. *Nestling:* Long grey-brown down, mouth reddish, gape pale yellow; leaves nest at about 16 days.

SEASON. Late April to early July; two broods.

YELLOW WAGTAIL *Motacilla flava* Plate 16
PGBB, p. 97, plate 35   [Wagtail Family

HABITAT AND RANGE. Most often in damp river valleys, water-meadows, sewage farms and fresh and salt-marshes, but also on dry heaths and commons, moorland and arable land under crops. Summer visitor, rather local, but common in E, SE and NW England, and almost absent from SW England and N and W Wales; in Scotland only in the Clyde valley; no longer breeds in Ireland. The Continental race, the blue-headed wagtail (*M. flava flava*) breeds occasionally in E and SE England, especially in SW Kent and SE Sussex.

NEST. Always in a hollow on the ground, normally well concealed by vegetation. Made of dried grass, etc. and usually lined with hair.

EGGS AND YOUNG. *Eggs:* 5–6; suffused and heavily sprinkled with yellowish-buff, occasionally greyish; occasional clutches hardly distinguishable from pied or grey wagtail's; incubation 12–13 days. *Nestling:* Buffish-white down, mouth orange-yellow, gape pale yellow; leaves nest at about 12 days. Ring number 1 overlapped.

SEASON. Mid-May to June in north, July in south; two broods normal in south, occasional in north.

BEARDED TIT *Panurus biarmicus* Plate 30   Tit Family
PGBB, p. 98, plate 17

HABITAT AND RANGE. Confined to sedge- and reed-beds on the Norfolk Broads and on some coastal marshes in E Anglia. Resident.

NEST. Always low down among reeds, sedge, or exceptionally other thick herbage. Made exclusively of immediately local materials, the lining being usually the dead flowerheads of the reeds.

EGGS AND YOUNG. *Eggs:* 5–7; white, streaked and flecked with brown; incubation 12–13 days. *Nestling:* No down; mouth red and black with two rows of white peg-like projections on either side of palate; tongue black with white tip and spurs; gape yellow; leaves nest at 10–11 days. Ring number 1 overlapped.

87

SEASON. April to July; two broods normal, sometimes three.

KINGFISHER *Alcedo atthis* Plate 8   Kingfisher Family
PGBB, p. 98, plate 20

HABITAT AND RANGE. Rivers, streams, canals and lakes. Resident throughout lowlands in England, Wales, Ireland and S Scotland.

NEST. Always in a hole, excavated usually in a river or canal bank, but occasionally in a sandy bank at some distance from water; exceptionally in other holes or cavities. Tunnel runs nearly horizontally for 18–36 inches into bank and ends in a round cavity, lined only with disgorged fish-bones. Entrance to tunnel always betrayed by 'whitewash' after young have hatched.

EGGS AND YOUNG. *Eggs:* 6–7; almost spherical, white, highly glossed; incubation about 20 days. *Nestling:* No down, mouth flesh-coloured, gape bluish-flesh; leaves nest at about 25 days. Ring size SO.

SEASON. April to August; two broods.

WATERSIDE BIRDS: Medium Short

GREY WAGTAIL *Motacilla cinerea* Plate 39
  PGBB, p. 99, plate 35   [Wagtail Family
HABITAT AND RANGE. Mainly swift rocky hill streams, but also
  locally near waterfalls, lashers and weirs on lowland rivers
  and streams, and occasionally lakes or tarns. Resident,
  common in all hill districts, but very local in N Scotland and
  local but increasing S and E of a line joining Humber and
  Lyme Regis.
NEST. Usually in a hole or on a ledge close to water, but
  occasionally at some distance from it; typical sites include
  ivy on or crevice in a lasher wall, ledge or deep crack in rock,
  inside boathouse, among roots of tree, old nest of dipper or
  other bird. Made of moss and other local materials, lined
  with hair.
EGGS AND YOUNG. *Eggs:* 5; buff sprinkled with rather indis-
  tinct grey-brown speckles; occasional clutches hardly distinguishable from pied or yellow wagtails'; incubation chiefly
  by hen, 12–13 days. *Nestling:* Longish golden-buff down,
  mouth orange, gape pale yellow; leaves nest at about 12 days.
  Ring number 1 overlapped.
SEASON. April to early June or July; two broods in some
  districts.

DIPPER *Cinclus cinclus* Plate 39   Dipper Family
  PGBB, p. 100, plate 39
HABITAT AND RANGE. Almost confined to swift hill streams,
  but sometimes on shores of hill lochs and in a few districts
  on lowland streams near weirs or lashers. Resident, common
  in almost all hill districts W and N of a line drawn from
  Lyme Regis through the Cotswolds to the Peak District, and
  thence to the Humber; very local on the E fringe of the
  breeding area, and breeds sporadically in the Midlands just
  E of it.
NEST. Always on a ledge or in a cavity over or very close to

water; typical sites are natural hole in river cliff, hole in mill wall, ledge under bridge, in ivy on tree or wall, among tree-roots; occasionally right under a waterfall, exceptionally on branch of tree. Domed nest, mainly built of moss and lined with dead leaves; like a large wren's nest; may be used again.

EGGS AND YOUNG. *Eggs:* 4–5; matt white; incubation by hen only, 16–17 days. *Nestling:* Long dark grey down, mouth orange-yellow, gape yellowish; leaves nest at about 23 days. Ring number 2 overlapped.

SEASON. Mid-March to June; two broods.

BAILLON'S CRAKE (*Porzana pusilla*), Plate 44; Rail Family (*PGBB*, p. 100, plate 36). Two or three pairs proved to have bred E Anglia, 1858, 1866 and 1889, but species so retiring that may well have bred elsewhere and at other times. Nest low down in thick vegetation in fens and swamps; eggs yellowish, spotted with yellow-brown. Two nests found in Norfolk in 1866 might possibly have belonged to Little Crake (*P. parva;* Plate 48) (*PGBB*, p. 100, plate 36), which has never been proved to breed in Britain. Nest, nest-site and eggs all closely resemble Baillon's Crake, but eggs slightly larger, paler and less glossy.

DUNLIN *Calidris alpina* Plate 18   Sandpiper Family
PGBB, p. 101, plates 37, 41, 79, 82

HABITAT AND RANGE. Grassy and peaty moorlands up to high altitudes, lowland peat-mosses and coastal marshes. Summer visitor, breeding on moors from Brecon and Derbyshire northwards, and on coast in S Lancashire and many parts of Scotland and Ireland; occasionally elsewhere.

NEST. Social; always in a scrape in the ground or a tussock of grass, lined with various local materials; usually in boggy place or near water.

EGGS AND YOUNG. *Eggs:* 4; pear-shaped, ground-colour varies widely, usually buff or olive-brown but sometimes blue-green, sprinkled with dark brown spots and blotches; incubation 21–22 days. *Chick:* Covered with buff down marbled

black; leaves nest within a few days. Ring number 1A.
SEASON. Mid-May to end June.

RINGED PLOVER *Charadrius hiaticula* Plate 18
PGBB, p. 103, plates 38, 79   [Plover Family

HABITAT AND RANGE. Mainly on sandy and pebbly beaches,
but also on arable land and other flat places near coast; in
some districts on sandy warrens and freshwater margins and
shoals far inland. Resident, common on all suitable coasts;
also breeds inland in Breckland (E Anglia) and parts of
N England, Scotland and Ireland.

NEST. Always in a scrape on the bare ground or very short
turf, with or without lining of local origin (on sand or
shingle, often small pebbles or shells).

EGGS AND YOUNG. *Eggs:* 4; pear-shaped; pale buff well
sprinkled with black spots; incubation 24–25 days. *Chick:*
Covered with yellowish or sandy grey down marked black
and dark brown; leaves nest within a few hours. Ring
number 1A.

SEASON. May to July; two broods.

JACK-SNIPE (*Lymnocryptes minimus*), Plate 48; Sandpiper
Family (*PGBB*, p. 103, plates 39, 78). Occasionally seen in
summer, and breeding has been suspected but never proved.
Eggs, laid on ground in swampy place, resemble common
snipe's.

COMMON SANDPIPER *Tringa hypoleucos* Plate 21
PGBB, p. 104, plates 39, 79   [Sandpiper Family

HABITAT AND RANGE. Beside streams, lochs (including sea-
lochs) and other waters in hilly districts, and sporadically by
lowland waters. Summer visitor, common in hill districts of
Scotland, Wales, N England and Ireland (not SE), sporadic
in S and E England.

NEST. Almost always on ground, usually among vegetation
and near water, a scrape lined with local materials.

EGGS AND YOUNG. *Eggs:* 4; pear-shaped, usually buffish but
sometimes greyish, marked with reddish-brown blotches;

incubation 21–22 days. *Chick:* Covered with grey-buff down marbled black and brown; leaves nest within a few hours. Ring number 1A.

SEASON. May and June.

WOOD-SANDPIPER (*Tringa glareola*), Plate 44; Sandpiper Family (*PGBB*, p. 104, plates 39, 80). Bred Northumberland 1853, Sutherland 1959 and Invernessshire 1960. Eggs very variable, but usually buffish marked brown, scarcely pear-shaped; nest normally on ground in open, but occasionally in tree in other birds' old nest.

PURPLE SANDPIPER (*Calidris maritima*), Plate 48; Sandpiper Family (*PGBB*, p. 105, plates 37, 79). Not infrequently summers in N Scotland (especially Shetland) and on Farne Islands, but never proved to have bred. Nest most likely to be found (if at all) on hilltops in far N Scotland; eggs not markedly pear-shaped, greenish at first then buff, marked dark brown.

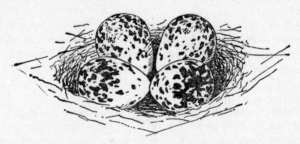

A TYPICAL WADER CLUTCH OF 4 EGGS WITH POINTED END INWARDS TO REDUCE BROODING SPACE TO MINIMUM.

GREEN SANDPIPER (*Tringa ochropus*), Plate 44; Sandpiper Family (*PGBB*, p. 105, plates 39, 40, 80). Bred Westmorland 1917, and Inverness-shire 1959. Nest more often in old nest of thrush or other bird in tree than on ground or anywhere else; eggs oval rather than pear-shaped, greenish or buffish with brown markings.

TURNSTONE (*Arenaria interpres*), Plate 48; Sandpiper Family (*PGBB*, p. 106, plates 38, 41, 79, 82). Regularly summers on most coasts British Isles, and breeding often suspected but never proved in N Scotland. Nest usually on ground on island; eggs oval rather than pear-shaped, mainly greenish with brown markings.

SPOTTED CRAKE *Porzana porzana* Plate 22 Rail Family *PGBB*, p. 107, plate 36

HABITAT AND RANGE. Swamps, fens, bogs and mosses, but especially swamps that are almost inaccessible owing to the spongy nature of the ground. Breeding range obscure, but summer visitor and has bred during past thirty years in Brecon, Cheshire, Dorset, Flint, Norfolk, Somerset, and probably Northumberland.

NEST. Usually in a tussock of sedge or tuft of grass; made of sedges, grasses and similar local materials.

EGGS AND YOUNG. *Eggs:* 8–12; like a small moorhen's (below), but usually rather more thickly speckled; incubation 19–20 days. *Chick:* Only distinguishable from water-rail by shorter bill; leaves nest soon after hatching. Ring number 2.

SEASON. Not adequately known, but seems to begin in mid- or late May; two broods on Continent, but insufficient information for Britain.

WATERSIDE BIRDS: Medium

BLACK TERN (*Chlidonias niger*), Plate 44; Gull Family (*PGBB*, p. 107, plates 102, 103). Formerly bred E. England, regularly till 1840's, sporadically till 1885, and again in Sussex in 1941–42. Nests colonially on ground near fresh water, or on floating waterweed; eggs buffish or greenish, strongly marked with dark brown.

LITTLE TERN *Sterna albifrons* Plate 25   Gull Family
    PGBB, p. 108, plates 60, 102
HABITAT AND RANGE. Shingle and sandy coasts, and marine islands; extremely rare inland. Summer visitor, scattered round whole coasts of British Isles, but absent or very local S Wales, N Scotland, S Ireland.
NEST. Colonial; nest a scrape in the ground, occasionally lined with small pebbles.
EGGS AND YOUNG. *Eggs:* 2–3; variable, but mostly buff ground-colour more or less heavily marked with greyish and dark brown spots and blotches; incubation 20–21 days. *Chick:* Covered with shortish down, sandy brown marbled black above, white below; leaves nest within a few hours. Ring number 1.
SEASON. Mid-May to mid-July.

COMMON SNIPE *Capella gallinago* Plate 21
    PGBB, p. 109, plates 39, 73, 78   [Sandpiper Family
HABITAT AND RANGE. All kinds of damp, marshy and boggy places inland, especially fields with many rushes. Resident, common over most of British Isles, but local in S England.
NEST. In a tussock of rushes, grass or sedge, usually near water; lined with grasses, etc.
EGGS AND YOUNG. *Eggs:* 4; pear-shaped, ground-colour variable but usually buff or olive, more or less heavily, and often spirally, blotched with dark brown; incubation by hen only, about 20 days. *Chick:* Covered with chestnut down marbled

black and sparsely spangled white; leaves nest within a few hours. Ring number 1A.

SEASON. April to May and June; sometimes two broods.

WATER-RAIL *Rallus aquaticus* Plate 22   Rail Family
PGBB, p. 110, plate 36

HABITAT AND RANGE. Swamps, fens, bogs and mosses in most parts of British Isles except W Scotland, but whether as resident or summer visitor obscure.

NEST. Always well concealed in vegetation on ground, on foundation of dead reeds or sedge, or in tussock of sedge or grass. Made of dead reeds, sedges and other local materials.

EGGS AND YOUNG. *Eggs:* 6–11; like a small moorhen's (p. 110) but covered to a greater extent with ashy-grey as well as brown spots and blotches; incubation 19–20 days. *Chick:* Covered with longish black down; leaves nest soon after hatching. Ring number 2.

SEASON. April to July; two broods.

RUFF (*Philomachus pugnax*), Plate 44; Sandpiper Family (*PGBB*, p. 111, plates 40, 42, 79, 82). Formerly bred in E England, regularly till 1871, sporadically till 1922; suspected since but never proved. Nest on ground in grass field, marshy or boggy place. Eggs hardly pear-shaped, very variable, but mainly buff marked brown.

COMMON REDSHANK *Tringa totanus* Plate 18
PGBB, p. 112, plates 40, 80, 81   [Sandpiper Family

HABITAT AND RANGE. All kinds of damp grassland, meadows, pastures, marshes and salt-marshes, often near lakes and rivers. Resident, common over most of British Isles, but not in Cornwall, Pembroke or parts of S Ireland.

NEST. Always in a scrape on ground, normally well hidden in a tuft or 'tent' of grass; lined with dried grass and similar materials.

EGGS AND YOUNG. *Eggs:* 4; usually pear-shaped, ground-colour very variable but mostly some shade of buff, more or less heavily spotted or blotched with dark reddish-brown;

incubation 22–23 days. *Chick:* Covered with buff down marbled black; leaves nest within a few hours. Ring number 1A.

SEASON. Mid-April to June.

GREENSHANK *Tringa nebularia* Plate 13 Sandpiper Family
PGBB, p. 113, plates 40, 43, 81

HABITAT AND RANGE. Moorland, with or without trees. Summer visitor to many parts of Scottish Highlands S to Argyll; in the islands regular only in Skye. Passage migrant elsewhere.

NEST. Always in a scrape on the ground, often near a stone or tree-stump; lined with various local materials.

EGGS AND YOUNG. *Eggs:* 4; pear-shaped; variable, but usually buff, beautifully marked with dark reddish-brown spots and blotches; incubation about 24 days. *Chick:* Covered with brown down marbled black; leaves nest within a few hours. Ring number 2.

SEASON. May and June.

ROCK-DOVE *Columba livia* Plate **9** Dove Family
PGBB, p. 113, plates 24, 68

HABITAT AND RANGE. Sea-cliffs in most parts of Scotland and Ireland, especially in N and NW and on isles; also local in Isle of Man.

NEST. Colonial; always on a ledge in a cave or in a crevice in a cliff; scanty material of local origin.

EGGS AND YOUNG. *Eggs:* 2; bluntly elliptical, white, slightly glossy; incubation about 18 days. *Nestling:* Sparse, hairy, yellowish down; leaves nest at about 36 days. Ring number 3.

SEASON. Throughout the year in parts of N Scotland, and perhaps elsewhere, but peak period probably April–May; two broods, often three.

LITTLE BITTERN (*Ixobrychus minutus*), Plate 45; Heron Family (*PGBB*, p. 114, plate 44). Has probably bred several times E Anglia and perhaps elsewhere E England. Nest, like common bittern's, normally on ground among reeds or other dense swampy vegetation, but occasionally in a tree; eggs matt white.

COMMON TERN *Sterna hirundo* Plate 20   Gull Family
PGBB, p. 115, plates 60, 102, 103

HABITAT AND RANGE. Mainly sandy and shingly sea-shores, also on grassy and rocky marine islands and by freshwater lochs, exceptionally inland at sewage farms, etc. Summer visitor to all coasts; inland often in Ireland and N Scotland, exceptionally in rest of Great Britain.

NEST. Colonial, often with arctic tern. Always a scrape in the ground; sometimes lined with various local materials.

EGGS AND YOUNG. *Eggs:* 3; buff or greyish with more or less heavy grey and brown markings; incubation about 24 days. *Chick:* Covered with pale buffish down marbled blackish-brown, often with black throat; leaves nest within a few hours. Ring number 1A.

SEASON. Mid-May to July.

ARCTIC TERN *Sterna macrura* Plate 20   Gull Family
PGBB, p. 116, plates 60, 103

HABITAT AND RANGE. Mainly sandy and shingly sea-shores, also on rocky islands in sea and by freshwater loughs. Summer visitor to all coasts and inland in Scotland and Ireland (commoner in W of both); in Wales only on islets of Anglesey; in England only on Farne Islands, and in NW England in any numbers, but odd pairs fairly regularly in Norfolk and Isle of Man.

NEST. Colonial, often with common tern, nest always a scrape on ground or in tuft of grass or rushes, often lined with sundry local materials.

EGGS AND YOUNG. *Eggs:* 2–3; not certainly distinguishable from common tern's (above), but tend to be more boldly marked and show greater variety and liveliness of colour; incubation 21–22 days. *Chick:* Not certainly distinguishable from common tern; leaves nest within a few hours. Ring number 1A.

SEASON. Late May to July.

THE POCKET GUIDE TO NESTS AND EGGS

ROSEATE TERN *Sterna dougallii* Plate 25   Gull Famiiy
PGBB, p. 116, plates 60, 103

HABITAT AND RANGE. Mainly sandy and shingly shores, also marine islands and exceptionally by fresh water. Summer visitor, mainly to shores of Irish Sea, where distinctly local; elsewhere a few odd pairs breed more or less regularly among other terns in Norfolk, Dorset, Farne Islands and Scilly Islands; colonies also in Donegal, Ayrshire and a few places on E coast Scotland.

NEST. Colonial, often with other terns; nest always in a hollow on ground; nest material infrequent.

EGGS AND YOUNG. *Eggs:* 1–2; buffish or whitish with dark reddish-brown markings; incubation about 24 days. *Chick:* Similar to common and arctic terns but can be told by coarse or matted appearance of down; leaves nest within a few hours. Ring number 2.

SEASON. June and July.

GULL-BILLED TERN (*Gelochelidon nilotica*), Plate 44; Gull Family (*PGBB*, p. 117, plate 103). Bred in Essex 1949–50. Nest on ground in salt-marshes or by saline, brackish or freshwater lagoons; eggs not unlike Sandwich tern's.

WATERSIDE BIRDS: Medium Long

STILT (*Himantopus himantopus*), Plate 44; Plover Family (*PGBB*, p. 117, plates 45, 83). Bred in Nottinghamshire in 1945. Nest on ground near shallow fresh water; eggs buffish spotted black.

WHIMBREL *Numenius phaeopus* Plate 13
PGBB, p. 118, plates 43, 81   [Sandpiper Family
HABITAT AND RANGE. Very local on moorland in the Shetlands, occasionally elsewhere in N Scotland.
NEST. Always in a scrape on the ground, scantily lined with various local materials.
EGGS AND YOUNG. *Eggs:* 4; like a small curlew's (below), but usually more heavily blotched; incubation about 24 days. *Chick:* Similar to curlew, but has two dark stripes on crown separated by a buff one; leaves nest within a few hours. Ring number 3.
SEASON. Late May and June.

BLACK-TAILED GODWIT *Limosa limosa* Plate 16
PGBB, p. 118, plates 42, 43, 81, 83   [Sandpiper Family
HABITAT AND RANGE. Grassy fields near water, also on dunes or moorland. Formerly bred widely in E England; shows increasing tendency to breed again: Lincolnshire 1940–41, Caithness 1946, Shetland 1949, and regularly at an unnamed locality since 1952.
NEST. Always in a scrape on ground, usually well hidden in thick grass; made of dead grasses, etc.
EGGS AND YOUNG. *Eggs:* 4; hardly pear-shaped, ground-colour varies from greenish through olive to brownish or buffish, more or less heavily blotched and spotted with brown; incubation 24 days. *Chick:* Covered with buff and pale cinnamon down marbled dark brown; leaves nest within a few hours. Ring number 3.
SEASON. May and June.

SANDWICH TERN *Sterna sandvicensis* Plate 25

PGBB, p. 119, plates 60, 102, 103   Gull Family

HABITAT AND RANGE. Mainly shingly and sandy sea-shores, also islands offshore and in freshwater loughs. Summer visitor, rather local; E Anglia, Farne Islands and NW England; Anglesey; coasts and islands of Galloway, Firth of Forth, Fife, Moray Firth and Orkney; in Ireland widespread but mainly in N and W.

NEST. Colonial; always a scrape on ground, sometimes lined with dried grass.

EGGS AND YOUNG. *Eggs:* 1–2; very variable, ground-colour anything from white to deep brown, more or less heavily spotted or blotched with darker brown; incubation 23 days. *Chick:* Covered with buffish or greyish down, having a matted appearance on upper parts; leaves nest in a few hours. Ring number 2.

SEASON. May and June.

AVOCET *Recurvirostra avosetta* Plate 25   Plover Family

PGBB, p. 120, plates 45, 83

HABITAT AND RANGE. Salt-marshes, brackish lagoons and grassy or sandy flats near coast. Formerly nested widely in E England; bred Ireland 1938, Norfolk 1943 and 1946, Essex 1944; has bred regularly in some numbers in Suffolk since 1947, latterly always at Havergate Island, a sanctuary of the Royal Society for the Protection of Birds.

NEST. Colonial. Always on the ground, often in a scrape lined with various local materials, sometimes building up to quite a substantial pile.

EGGS AND YOUNG. *Eggs:* 4; mostly pale buff, blotched and spotted with grey or dark brown; incubation about 23 days. *Chick:* Covered with greyish-buff down marbled blackish-brown; beak straight for first week; leaves nest within a few hours. Ring number 2.

SEASON. Late April to July.

OYSTERCATCHER *Haematopus ostralegus* Plate 18

PGBB, p. 120, plates 45, 83   Plover Family

HABITAT AND RANGE. Flat, shingly, rocky, sandy or grassy

places near the sea, also on cliff-tops, marine islands and in the north inland on shingly and grassy places near water, on moorland and even in arable fields. Resident, common on coasts of Scotland, Wales and Ireland, also on W coast and sparingly on S and E coasts England; inland in many parts of Scotland, less commonly in N England and sporadically in Ireland.

NEST. Always a scrape on ground, with or without local nesting materials, which on shingle may include small shells and pebbles, and on turf rabbit droppings.

EGGS AND YOUNG. *Eggs:* 2–3; usually pale buff, spotted, blotched or streaked with dark brown; incubation 26–27 days. *Chick:* Covered with buff and greyish down marbled black; leaves nest within a few hours. Ring number 3.

SEASON. Mid-April to July.

MARSH-HARRIER *Circus aeruginosus* Plate 22
PGBB, p. 121, plates 32, 74   [Hawk Family

HABITAT AND RANGE. Extensive tracts of reeds and marshland. Summer visitor, very local in E Anglia, recently attempting to establish itself in SE England, N Wales, and perhaps elsewhere. Formerly also bred Ireland and more widely in England.

NEST. Always on ground among thick aquatic vegetation; a substantial pile of such vegetation, much larger than Montagu's harrier's, lined with grasses.

EGGS AND YOUNG. *Eggs:* 4–5; bluish-white, matt; incubation mainly by hen, about 36 days. *Nestling:* Largely covered with whitish and buffish down; leaves nest after about 37–38 days, before it can fly. Ring number 3.

SEASON. Late April to July.

OSPREY (*Pandion haliaetus*), Plate 46; Osprey Family
(*PGBB*, p. 122, plates 32, 74). Formerly bred on many lochs in Scottish Highlands down to 1916; bred Spey Valley unsuccessfully 1955-58, successfully 1959-60. Nest a bulky pile of sticks in a tree or on ground on island; eggs white with red-brown blotches.

WATERSIDE BIRDS: Long

CURLEW *Numenius arquata* Plate 18   Sandpiper Family
  PGBB, p. 124, plates 43, 81, 107

HABITAT AND RANGE. Many kinds of more or less damp open
  country, moors, bogs, swampy lowland heaths, valley grassland, sand-dunes. Resident, common throughout most of
  British Isles, but very local in E and SE England and
  Midlands.

NEST. Always in a scrape on the ground or in a tussock, lined
  with dried grass and other local materials.

EGGS AND YOUNG. *Eggs:* 4; hardly pear-shaped, various
  shades of buff, brown and olive, spotted and blotched with
  darker brown; incubation 29–30 days. *Chick:* Covered with
  buff down marbled blackish-brown; leaves nest within a few
  hours. Ring number 3.

SEASON. Late April to July.

CURLEW CHICK

WATERSIDE BIRDS: Very Long

GREYLAG GOOSE *Anser anser* Plate 17   Duck Family
PGBB, p. 128, plates 57, 95

HABITAT AND RANGE. Moorland, especially with scattered lochs, and marine islands. Resident, very local and decreasing in N Scotland and Hebrides; full-winged birds exist in private collections in E Anglia, Gloucestershire, W Ross, Sutherland and Co. Fermanagh.

NEST. Nearly always in a hollow on the ground in long heather; made of various local materials, lined with feathers (white with greyish centres) and down (grey with pale centres). Eggs covered with down during bird's absence.

EGGS AND YOUNG. *Eggs:* 4–6; elliptical, whitish, often stained yellow or brownish in nest; incubation by goose only, 27–28 days. *Gosling:* Covered with olive-brown and yellowish down; leaves nest within a few hours. Ring size 19 mm.

SEASON. Late April to June.

SEA-EAGLE (*Haliæëtus albicilla*), Plate 46; Hawk Family (*PGBB*, p. 129, plates 34, 77). Formerly bred widely round coast, but not since 1908, and seems less likely to re-establish itself than most lost species. Nest a pile of sticks, often immense, on a cliff ledge; egg white.

BITTERN *Botaurus stellaris* Plate 22   Heron Family
PGBB, p. 129, plates 44, 74, 85

HABITAT AND RANGE. Extensive reed-beds, swamps and fens. Resident, local in E Anglia, Lincolnshire, and perhaps one or two other counties in England.

NEST. Always on ground or over water in thick aquatic vegetation, an untidy pile of dead sedges, etc.

EGGS AND YOUNG. *Eggs:* 4–6; elliptical, olive-brown, matt; incubation by hen alone, about 25 days. *Nestling:* Sparsely covered with long reddish and buffish down; leaves nest in

about 18 days, before it can fly. Ring size 16 mm.
SEASON. April to June.

SPOONBILL (*Platalea leucorodia*), Plate 46; Spoonbill Family
(*PGBB*, p. 130, plates 45, 86). Bred in various parts of
England and Wales till seventeenth century; summering
birds especially in E England have often given rise to hope
that it might breed again. Colonial; nest most likely to be
on ground in reed-bed, but might be in bush or tree near
water. Eggs white sparsely marked red-brown.

HERON   *Ardea cinerea*   Plate 36   Heron Family
   PGBB, p. 131, plates 76, 84, 85
HABITAT AND RANGE. Heronries, usually in trees near water,
   but occasionally away from water, in small woods, in reed-
   beds, or even on cliffs, may be situated in almost any kind of
   country. Resident, scattered over almost whole of British
   Isles, though local.
NEST. Colonial; nearly always in a tree, but occasionally on
   ground in reed-bed or on cliff-ledge. A substantial pile of
   sticks or reeds lined with various local materials. Except for
   rook, the only common colonial bird making big stick nests
   in trees.
EGGS AND YOUNG. *Eggs:* 3–5; elliptical, greenish-blue, matt;
   incubation about 25 days. *Nestling:* Fairly well covered
   with greyish-brown down, head adorned with long whitish
   halo-like bristles; leaves nest at 7–8 weeks. Ring size 16
   mm., to be used till young bird well feathered.
SEASON. February to June; occasionally a second brood.

WATERSIDE BIRDS: Huge

COMMON CRANE (*Megalornis grus*), Plate 46; Crane
Family. Bred in E Anglia till about 1600, and seems unlikely
ever to return. Huge nest on ground in bog or swamp, egg
variable in colour but unspotted.

YOUNG CRANE

WATER BIRDS: Short

STORM-PETREL *Hydrobates pelagicus* Plates 2, 9
  PGBB, p. 132, plates, 97, 98   Storm-Petrel Family
HABITAT AND RANGE. Marine islands off coasts of Cornwall, Pembrokeshire, Ireland and W and N Scotland.
NEST. Social; in burrow in turf, or well concealed among large stones or boulders, or occasionally in drystone wall or ruined building. Either no nest material or a few scraps of dried grass, etc.
EGGS AND YOUNG. *Eggs:* 1; bluntly elliptical, white; incubation about 41 days. *Nestling:* Covered with silvery-grey down becoming brown; does not leave nest for about 9 weeks. Ring number 1A overlapped.
SEASON. June to September.

RED-NECKED PHALAROPE *Phalaropus lobatus* Plate 21
  PGBB, p. 133, plates 46, 79, 101   [Sandpiper Family
HABITAT AND RANGE. Coastal or loch-side areas with scattered freshwater pools and boggy patches. Summer visitor, very local in N and W isles of Scotland, and in one or two localities in NW Ireland.
NEST. Social; always in a scrape on ground or in tussock of grass, and close to water; lined with grasses, etc.
EGGS AND YOUNG. *Eggs:* 4; pear-shaped, like miniature red-shank's eggs; incubation by cock only, about 20 days. *Chick:* Covered with various shades of buff down marbled black; leaves nest within a few hours. Ring number 1A.
SEASON. Late May to early July.

WATER BIRDS: Medium Short

FORK-TAILED PETREL *Oceanodroma leucorrhoa* Plate 2
PGBB, p. 133, plates 97, 98 [Storm-Petrel Family
HABITAT AND RANGE. A handful of semi-oceanic islands; only
known on St. Kilda, N Rona, Sula Sgeir and Flannan Isles
(Outer Hebrides); has bred on islets off W coast Ireland.
NEST. Social; in burrow in turf or well concealed among large
stones or boulders, or occasionally in drystone wall or ruined
building. Local nest materials, if any.
EGGS AND YOUNG. *Eggs:* 1; larger than storm-petrel's (above)
and usually finely spotted red-brown at one end; incubation
probably at least 50 days. *Nestling:* Covered with greyish
sooty-brown down; does not leave nest for well over 50
days. Ring number 1A overlapped.
SEASON. June to September.

STORM-PETREL CHICK

WATER BIRDS: Medium

MANX SHEARWATER *Procellaria puffinus* Plate **2**
  PGBB, p. 135, plates 97, 98   [Shearwater Family
HABITAT AND RANGE. Marine islands and oceanic headlands
  off W coasts Great Britain and Ireland. Local, but colonies
  usually large; also visits and occasionally breeds on mainland cliffs (has bred recently Co. Durham).
NEST. Colonial; always in a burrow. Nest, of a few grasses
  and other local materials, usually at least three feet into
  burrow.
EGGS AND YOUNG. *Eggs:* 1; matt white; incubation about 53
  days. *Nestling:* Covered with long grey-brown down; leaves
  burrow at 10–11 weeks, nearly a fortnight after fledging.
  Double-ended ring.
SEASON. May to September.

DABCHICK *Podiceps ruficollis* Plate 27   Grebe Family
  PGBB, p. 135, plates 46, 47, 49, 89
HABITAT AND RANGE. All kinds of fresh water, ponds, lakes
  and slow-moving rivers; sometimes in town parks. Resident,
  common almost throughout British Isles.
NEST. Sometimes social; a pile of waterweed, usually surrounded by water, but always either grounded on or anchored
  to aquatic vegetation. Eggs are covered up when bird leaves
  nest.
EGGS AND YOUNG. *Eggs:* 4–6; elliptical, white when first laid
  but soon becoming stained buff or red-brown; incubation
  19–20 days. *Chick:* Covered with down, general appearance
  blackish-brown with rufous streaks; can swim almost at
  birth and leaves nest within a few hours. Ring number 3
  overlapped; must not be ringed till fairly well feathered.
SEASON. April to July, but occasionally as early as February
  and as late as September; two broods, perhaps sometimes
  three.

PUFFIN *Fratercula arctica* Plate 2   Auk Family
  PGBB, p. 137, plates 59, 97, 99, 100
HABITAT AND RANGE. Cliff-bound coasts and marine islands.
  Breeds locally round British and Irish coasts, but not
  between Flamborough Head and Isle of Wight.
NEST. Colonial. Usually in a burrow in turf, but sometimes in
  a cavity under a rock, on seaward slopes and islands; exceptionally in high dunes. No nest material in ordinary sense,
  but bits of grass, etc. are scattered in the nesting tunnel.
EGGS AND YOUNG. *Eggs:* 1; white with brownish markings
  which may or may not be visible beneath the thick chalky
  covering; incubation 41–42 days. *Nestling:* Thickly covered
  with long soft brownish down, white on belly; leaves nest at
  about 7 weeks. Double-ended ring, but must not be ringed
  till fairly well feathered.
SEASON. Last few days of April till August.

BLACK-NECKED GREBE *Podiceps caspicus* Plate 27
  PGBB, p. 137, plates 46, 99   [Grebe Family
HABITAT AND RANGE. Lochs, lakes or reservoirs with some
  vegetation growing in the water at the edge. Breeds irregularly in various parts of British Isles, but colonies rarely last
  long, and breeding status since 1940 obscure. During
  1920–50 bred at times in Somerset, Hertfordshire, Norfolk,
  Cheshire, Yorkshire and Westmorland; Anglesey; Mid-
  lothian, Perth, Fife, and perhaps elsewhere; Co. Ros-
  common, a colony of some 250 pairs 1929–33, but only
  sporadically before and after.
NEST. Sometimes colonial; otherwise similar to dabchick
  (above).
EGGS AND YOUNG. *Eggs:* 3–4; similar to dabchick's but
  larger; incubation 20–21 days. *Chick:* Covered with blackish
  down indistinctly striped whitish—no trace of dabchick's
  rufous colouring; can swim almost at birth and leaves nest
  within a few hours. Ring number 4, but must not be ringed
  till fairly well feathered.
SEASON. Mid-May to July; perhaps sometimes a second brood.

THE POCKET GUIDE TO NESTS AND EGGS

SLAVONIAN GREBE *Podiceps auritus* Plate 27
PGBB, p. 137, plates 46, 99   [Grebe Family

HABITAT AND RANGE. Lochs with some vegetation growing in water at edge. Very local in Inverness and Sutherland.

NEST. Semi-colonial; partial to small bays partly overgrown with horsetail and other upright vegetation; otherwise similar to dabchick (above).

EGGS AND YOUNG. *Eggs:* 4; similar to dabchick's and black-necked grebe's, but slightly larger than latter and tends to be a little more pointed; incubation about 23 days. *Chick:* Similar to black-necked grebe, but stripes on head, neck and upper parts much more distinct, and more as in great crested grebe, can swim almost from birth and leaves nest within a few hours. Ring number 4, but must not be ringed till fairly well feathered.

SEASON. Late May to July; perhaps sometimes a second brood.

MOORHEN *Gallinula chloropus* Plates 22, 27, 32
PGBB, p. 138, plates 36, 87   [Rail Family

HABITAT AND RANGE. All kinds of fresh water with plenty of thick herbage for cover, especially ponds, slow-moving rivers, marshes and sewage farms; plentiful in town parks. Resident, common almost throughout British Isles.

NEST. Commonest site is among sedge, reed-mace and other thick aquatic vegetation in or by side of pond, lake or river, but also not infrequently up to 15 feet up in a tree, bush or hedge either overhanging water or up to a quarter of a mile away from it; exceptionally in old nest of other bird. Nest made of dried blades of various aquatic plants, or of other local materials when away from water, and decorated with fresh greenery during incubation; nests in thick vegetation may be tented over.

EGGS AND YOUNG. *Eggs:* 5–8; pale buff, usually plentifully sprinkled with red-brown spots and specks; incubation 20–21 days. *Chick:* Covered with thick black down with whitish marks on head which distinguish it from young coot which has most of head bright rufous; bill red, bare crown blue:

leaves nest within 2–3 days and can swim at once. Ring number 4, but must not be ringed till fairly well feathered.

SEASON. March–April to August or September, but eggs or young may occur exceptionally in almost any month; two broods, often three.

BLACK GUILLEMOT *Uria grylle* Plate 9   Auk Family
PGBB, p. 139, plates 59, 87, 99, 100

HABITAT AND RANGE. Sea-cliffs and islands in sea-lochs and open sea. Resident, scattered round N and W coasts and islands of Scotland, Ireland (especially N and W coasts), Isle of Man, and St. Bees Head, Cumberland; has bred Bempton cliffs, Yorkshire, and Anglesey.

NEST. Social, usually in a crevice in a cliff or among boulders, occasionally in ruined wall or building, or in burrow. Never on open ledge like common guillemot. No nest material.

EGGS AND YOUNG. *Eggs:* 1–2; shaped like gulls' not pear-shaped like common guillemot's, whitish ground-colour variously tinted buff or bluish-green and more or less heavily blotched blackish- or reddish-brown and grey; incubation about 28 days. *Nestling:* Thickly covered with soft, blackish-brown down; leaves nest at about 35 days. Ring number 3, but must not be ringed till fairly well feathered.

SEASON. May to early August.

TEAL *Anas crecca* Plate 16   Duck Family
PGBB, p. 140, plates 47, 49, 90

HABITAT AND RANGE. Woods, heaths, bogs, marshes and neighbourhood of fresh water. Resident, fairly common over most of British Isles, but local in S England.

NEST. Always in a scrape on the ground well concealed by thick vegetation, often near water but equally often well away from it. Lined with various local materials mixed with feathers (grey-brown and whitish) and down (dark with pale centres). Eggs covered with down in bird's absence.

EGGS AND YOUNG. *Eggs:* 8–10; elliptical, pale buffish often with a greenish tinge; incubation by duck only, 21–22 days. *Duckling:* Similar to mallard (below) but much smaller;

111

THE POCKET GUIDE TO NESTS AND EGGS

leaves nest within a few hours, can swim almost from birth. Ring number 3 overlapped, but must not be ringed till fairly well feathered.

SEASON. Mid-April to June.

BLACK-HEADED GULL *Larus ridibundus* Plates 20, 27
  PGBB, p. 141, plates 60, 61, 62, 101, 104,   [Gull Family
  105, 107

HABITAT AND RANGE. Moors, bogs, islands in lochs and lakes, sand-dunes, shingle-banks, marshes and sewage farms. Resident, common over most of Scotland, Ireland, N and Mid-Wales and N England, more sparingly on E and S coasts England and shores of Bristol Channel, and inland in isolated colonies in Middlesex, Northants, Cambridge and Norfolk.

NEST. Colonial; site variable, but almost always either on ground or (very commonly) on tuft of rushes or sedges; sometimes a rather grebe-like floating nest; exceptionally in a bush or tree or on a building. Nest usually a substantial pile of local dried vegetation, contrasting especially with terns' nests when seen among them on sand or shingle.

EGGS AND YOUNG. *Eggs:* 3; very variable, ranging from deep brown through pale buff to pale bluish-green, more or less heavily spotted and blotched with dark brown; incubation about 23 days. *Chick:* Covered with brown down marbled blackish; leaves nest within a few hours. Ring number 3 overlapped, but must not be ringed till fairly well feathered.

SEASON. Mid-April to July; no second brood, but repeat clutches exceptionally numerous owing to habitual robbery of nests at many colonies.

SNOW BUNTING ♀

COMMON REDSTART ♀

WHEATEAR

COAL-TIT

STOCK-DOVE

LITTLE OWL

(Burrows shown excavated)

STORM-PETREL

FORK-TAILED PETREL

MANX
SHEARWATER

PUFFIN

SHELD-DUCK

ROCK-PIPIT

Nests in Holes in Ground by S

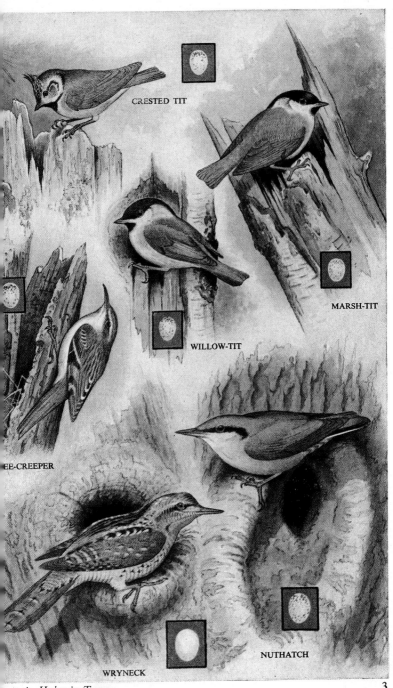

CRESTED TIT

MARSH-TIT

WILLOW-TIT

EE-CREEPER

WRYNECK

NUTHATCH

ests in Holes in Trees

3

TAWNY OWL

BARRED WOODPECKER

PIED
WOODPECK

HOOPOE

GREEN WOODPECKER

Nests in Holes in Tr

COAL-TIT

BLUE TIT

WRYNECK

GREAT TIT

REDSTART

TREE-SPARROW

PIED FLYCATCHER

Nests in Holes in Trees, Walls, Cliffs or Steep Banks   5

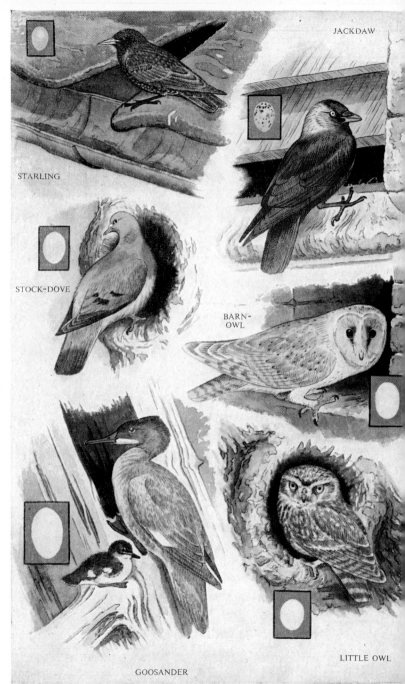

JACKDAW

STARLING

STOCK-DOVE

BARN-OWL

GOOSANDER

LITTLE OWL

Nests in Holes in Trees, Walls, Cliffs or Steep Bank

BLACK REDSTART

ROBIN

PIED WAGTAIL

SPOTTED
FLYCATCHER

HOUSE-SPARROW

SAND MARTIN

KINGFISHER

CHOUGH

SWIF

RED-BREASTED MERGANSER

Nests in Holes in Walls, Steep Banks and Cliffs (Inlan

CHOUGH

ROCK-DOVE

ROCK-PIPIT

BLACK GUILLEMOT

SAND-MARTIN

STORM-PETREL

RAZORBILL

WILLOW-WARBLER

WOOD-WARBLER

ROBIN

NIGHTINGALE

STONECHAT

WHINCHAT

Nests on Ground (Lan

CUCKOO
laying egg in Meadow Pipit's nest

WOODLARK

EE PIPIT

LARK

YELLOW HAMMER

CORN BUNTING

sts on Ground (Land)   11

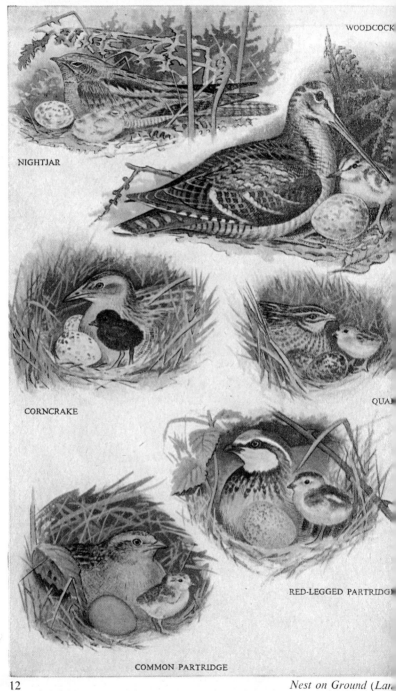

WOODCOCK

NIGHTJAR

CORNCRAKE

QUAIL

RED-LEGGED PARTRIDGE

COMMON PARTRIDGE

Nest on Ground (Lar

DOTTEREL (♂)

GOLDEN PLOVER

WHIMBREL

GREENSHANK

RING-OUZEL

STONE-CURLEW

HEN HARRIER

MERLIN

SHORT-EARED OWL

LONG-EARED OWL

HOODED CROW

Nests on Ground (Lan

PTARMIGAN

BLACK GROUSE

RED GROUSE

CAPERCAILLIE

LAPWING

BLACK-TAILED
GODWIT

TEAL

YELLOW WAGTAIL

Nests on Ground on Land or by Fresh Wat

MONTAGU'S HARRIER

PHEASANT

SHOVELER

WIGEON

GREY LAG GOOSE

Nests on Ground away from, or by Fresh Water

17

COMMON
REDSHANK

OYSTERCATCHER

RINGED PLOVER

CURLEW

DUNLIN

Nests on Ground on Land, by Fresh Water or by Se

ARCTIC SKUA

LESSER BLACK-BACK

GREAT BLACK-BACK

MALLARD

COMMON TERN

ARCTIC TERN

BLACK-HEADED GULL

COMMON GULL

RED-BREASTED MERGANSER

Nests on Ground by Se

LITTLE RINGED PLOVER

COMMON SANDPIPER

TEMMINCK'S STINT

RED-NECKED
PHALAROPE (♂)

COMMON SNIPE

SPOTTED CRAKE

MOORHEN

MARSH-HARRIER

WATER-RAIL

BITTERN

Nests on Ground by Fresh Water

PINTAIL

GADWALL

COMMON POCHARD

GARGANEY

TUFTED DUCK

COMMON SCOTER

RED-THROATED DIVER

BLACK-THROATE
DIVER

CANADA GOOSE

MUTE SWAN

WHOOPER SWAN

Nests on Ground by Fresh Wate

KENTISH PLOVER

LITTLE TERN

ROSEATE TERN

SANDWICH TERN

ROCK PIPIT

AVOCET

EIDER

GREAT SKUA

CORMORAN[T]

GANNET

Nests on Ground by Se

DABCHICK

BLACK-NECKED GREBE

VONIAN GREBE

GREAT CRESTED
GREBE

OOT

MOORHEN

BLACK-HEADED
GULL

ts Floating on or Surrounded by Fresh Water

CIRL-BUNTING

YELLOWHAMM

CORN BUNTING

LINNET

DARTFORD WARBLER

TWI

STONECHAT

WHINCHAT

Nests in Herbage or Low Bushes (Lo

REN

CHIFFCHAFF

LESSER WHITETHROAT

HEDGE-SPARROW

COMMON WHITETHROAT

GARDEN-WARBLER

BLACKCAP

sts in Herbage or Low Bushes (Land)   29

REED-WARBLER
with Cuckoo's egg

MARSH-WARBLER

SEDGE-WARBLER

GRASSHOPPER-WARBLER

REED-BUNTING

BEARDED TIT

Nests in Herbage or Low Bushes (Land and/or Wate

LESSER REDPOLL

LINNET

LONG-TAILED TIT

CHAFFINCH

BULLFINCH

GREENFINCH

sts in Bushes or Trees (high or low) 31

RED-BACKED SHRIKE

BLACKBIRD

SONG-THRUSH

REDWING

TURTLE-DOVE

MOORHEN

32

Nests in Bushes or Trees (high or

GOLDCREST

GOLDFINCH

HOUSE-SPARROW

SISKIN

HAWFINCH

CROSSBILL

GOLDEN ORIOLE

MAGPIE

JAY

WOOD PIGEON

ROOK

LONG-EARED OWL

Nests in Trees or Tall Bushes

KITE

HONEY-BUZZARD

GOSHAWK

SPARROWHAWK

HOBBY

HERON

MALLARD

MANDARIN
DUCK

EGYPTIAN GOOSE

Nests in Trees and Tall Bushes (by Wate

MERLIN

KESTREL

VREN

SPOTTED
FLYCATCHER

HOODED *and* CARRION-CROWS
Mixed pair where ranges overlap

RAVEN

PEREGRINE

COMMON
BUZZARD

GOLDEN EAGLE

Nests in or against Trees or Cliffs

HOUSE MARTIN

SWALLOW

BLACK
REDSTART

PIED WAGTAIL
with Cuckoo's egg

GREY WAGTAIL

DIPPER

Nests on Ledges on Cliffs or Buildings   39

CARRION-CROW

LONDON PIGEON

KESTREL

BARN-OWL

LITTLE OWL

Nests on Ledges on Cliffs or Building

KITTIWAKE

HERRING-GULL

FULMAR

GANNET

GUILLEMOT

RAZORBILL

SHAG

CORMORANT

Nests on Ledges on Sea C

BRAMBLING

ICTERINE WARBLER

SAVI'S WARBLER

MOUSTACHED
WARBLER

TAWNY PIPIT

GREEN SANDPIPER

WOOD-SANDPIPER

REEVE
(female R

STILT

BAILLON'S CRAK

BLACK TERN

GULL-BILLED TERN

Nests of Former or Exceptional Bre

LONG-TAILED DUCK

GOLDENEYE

SCAUP

RED-CRESTED POCHARD

LITTLE
BITTERN

PALLAS'S SAND-GROUSE

SEA-EAGLE

OSPREY

GREAT BUSTARD

WHITE STORK

COMMON CRANE

SPOONBILL

Nests of Former or Exceptional Bree

FIRECREST

SERIN

GREAT
BLACK
WOODPECKER

FIELDFARE

BEE -
EATER

EASTERN
COLLARED DOVE

WOODCHAT

s of Birds which May Have Bred or May Breed in Future

47

PURPLE SANDPIPER

TURNSTONE

JACK-SNIPE

VELVET SCOTER

GREAT NORTHERN DIVER

Nests of Birds which May Have Bred or May Breed in Fr

WATER BIRDS: Medium Long

COOT *Fulica atra* Plate 27 Rail Family
PGBB, p. 141, plates 36, 87, 92, 99

HABITAT AND RANGE. Similar to moorhen (above), but favours rather larger inland waters and less partial to rivers; requires a fringe of thick vegetation at water's edge; sometimes in town parks. Resident, common throughout British Isles.

NEST. Semi-colonial, either surrounded by water or in swamp, often in a tuft of rushes, sometimes floating like a grebe, or on a half-submerged bough. Nest a substantial pile of dried sedge, water-weeds, etc., sometimes built up so high as to conceal the sitting bird.

EGGS AND YOUNG. *Eggs:* 5–10; larger than moorhen's, less buff and more stone in ground-colour, and with smaller spots of a darker brown; incubation 22–23 days. *Chick:* Covered with blackish down, tipped rufous about head and neck, which distinguishes it at once from moorhen, leaves nest within 3–4 days, when can swim, but returns there to roost at night. Ring number 4 overlapped, but must not be ringed till fairly well feathered.

SEASON. Mid-March to August; two broods, sometimes three.

GARGANEY *Anas querquedula* Plate 23 Duck Family
PGBB, p. 142, plates 47, 49, 90, 92

HABITAT AND RANGE. Neighbourhood of marshes and fresh water. Summer visitor, breeding locally in Cambridgeshire and coastal counties from Norfolk to Dorset, and occasionally elsewhere in England, mainly in S, but range apparently extending.

NEST. Always in hollow on ground, in thick cover, usually long grass in hayfield, but also rough herbage near water. Nest lined with dried grasses, feathers and down, which can both at once be told from teal's by pure white tips. Eggs covered with down in bird's absence.

EGGS AND YOUNG. *Eggs:* 10–11; elliptical, creamy-buff, never with greenish tinge of some teal eggs, but best identified by characteristic down; incubation by duck only, about 22 days. *Duckling:* Very similar to teal; leaves nest within a few hours. Ring number 3 overlapped, but must not be ringed till fairly well feathered.

SEASON. Late April to June.

COMMON GULL *Larus canus* Plate 20   Gull Family
  PGBB, p. 144, plates 61, 62, 101, 104, 107

HABITAT AND RANGE. Moors, bogs, islands in lochs, marshes, sea-cliffs, sand-dunes and shingle banks. Resident, common in Scotland (except SE) and W coast Ireland (Donegal to Kerry); in England a small isolated colony at Dungeness (Kent).

NEST. Colonial, either on ground or on ledges of rocky stacks offshore; exceptionally in such sites as tree-stump or old nest of other bird. Nest made of local materials.

EGGS AND YOUNG. *Eggs:* 3; like a small herring-gull's (below), but usually less heavily spotted; incubation 22–23 days. *Chick:* Similar to black-headed gull, but contrast of dark and light more marked; leaves nest within a day or two. Ring number 3, but must not be ringed till fairly well feathered.

SEASON. Mid-May to June or July.

KITTIWAKE *Rissa tridactyla* Plate 41   Gull Family
  PGBB, p. 145, plates 61, 101, 104, 105

HABITAT AND RANGE. Sea-cliffs and marine islands. Very local on NE, SW and NW coasts England and in Wales and Isle of Man, local on Scottish coasts, more commonly round Irish coasts.

NEST. Colonial; almost always on ledge on sea-cliff or inside sea-cave, very exceptionally on a building or on ground on sand-dunes. Unlike most other cliff-nesting sea-birds makes a cup-shaped nest of seaweed and other local materials.

EGGS AND YOUNG. *Eggs:* 2–3; ground-colour varies from pale blue-grey to buffish and brown, with grey and brown spots and blotches; incubation 22–23 days. *Chick:* Covered with longish down, creamy-white on head and neck, grey-brown

114

on upper parts, white underneath; leaves nest at 44–45 days. Ring number 3, but must not be ringed till fairly well feathered.

SEASON. Late May to July.

RAZORBILL *Alca torda* Plates 9, 42   Auk Family
PGBB, p. 143, plates 59, 97, 99, 100

HABITAT AND RANGE. Sea-cliffs and rocky marine islands, all round coasts of British Isles, but not between Flamborough Head and the Needles.

NEST. Social; no nest material, egg being laid on bare rock, usually in a cavity or under a boulder towards the top of the cliff, but sometimes on open ledge like a guillemot.

EGGS AND YOUNG. *Eggs:* 1; can be told at once from guillemot's by ovate, not pear-shaped, appearance; variable (but less so than guillemot's), ground-colour almost any shade of brown, buff, cream, white or blue-green, fairly heavily spotted and blotched in colours ranging from brown to black; incubation about 35 days. *Nestling:* Covered with white, buff and blackish-brown down; leaves nest at 15–16 days. Double-ended ring, but must not be ringed till fairly well feathered.

SEASON. Mid-May to early August.

GUILLEMOT *Uria aalge* Plate 42   Auk Family
PGBB, p. 146, plates 59, 97, 99, 100

HABITAT AND RANGE. Sea-cliffs with ledges all round coasts of British Isles, but not between Flamborough Head and the Needles.

NEST. Colonial; always on narrow cliff ledges or on flat top of offshore stack; never in a crevice like razorbill; no nest material.

EGGS AND YOUNG. *Eggs:* 1; markedly pear-shaped; ground-colour more variable than that of any other British bird, almost any shade of blue-green, brown, yellow, buff or white; some very heavily blotched and spotted with various shades of yellow, brown and black; others quite lightly spotted, streaked, scrawled or scribbled with these colours; not

115

infrequently no, or next to no, markings at all; incubation about 36 days. *Nestling:* Covered with black, white, grey and brownish down; leaves ledge at about 16 days. Double-ended ring, but must not be ringed till fairly well feathered.
SEASON. Mid-May to early August.

TUFTED DUCK *Aythya fuligula* Plate 23   Duck Family
PGBB, p. 146, plates 51, 88, 90, 93
HABITAT AND RANGE. Inland waters with plenty of thick cover round them. Resident, local throughout British Isles but only sporadically on W coast Great Britain and SE Ireland.
NEST. Well hidden in hollow on ground in thick vegetation, especially tuft of rushes, always near and often very close to water. Nest of grasses and other local materials, lined with down, which is dark and sooty, and whitish feathers; often a tent of grass-stems overhead. Eggs covered with down in bird's absence.
EGGS AND YOUNG. *Eggs:* 6–14; elliptical, grey-green, matt; incubation by duck only, about 24 days. *Duckling:* Covered with blackish-brown down with some yellowish patches on under parts; leaves nest shortly after birth and can swim, and even dive, when a few hours old. Ring number 3, but must not be ringed till fairly well feathered.
SEASON. Mid-May to early July.

MANDARIN DUCK *Aix galericulata* Plate 36
PGBB, p. 147, plates 52, 54   [Duck Family
HABITAT AND RANGE. Freshwater lakes surrounded by woods and shrubberies with scattered small ponds and streams, and surrounding farmland. Resident (introduced) in Berkshire (Virginia Water), Surrey (Cobham area), Bedfordshire (Woburn) and Shropshire.
NEST. Always in a hole or hollow in a tree, not necessarily in a wood or very close to water. Nest lined with rotten wood and white down. Eggs covered with down in bird's absence.
EGGS AND YOUNG. *Eggs:* 9–12; elliptical, pale buff, glossy; incubation by duck only, about 29 days. *Duckling:* Covered with buff down marbled brown; leaves nest soon after

116

hatching. Ring number 4, but must not be ringed till fairly well feathered.

SEASON. April and May.

LONG-TAILED DUCK (*Clangula hyemalis*), Plate 45; Duck Family (*PGBB*, p. 148, plates 88, 92). Proved to have bred Orkney 1911, and has probably bred both Orkney and Shetland on a number of other occasions. Nest on ground not far from water; eggs olive or yellowish.

ARCTIC SKUA *Stercorarius parasiticus* Plate 19
PGBB, p. 150, plates 63, 106 [Skua Family

HABITAT AND RANGE. Barren moorlands in Caithness and on Scottish isles from Inner Hebrides northwards. Otherwise coastal passage migrant.

NEST. Social. Always on the ground, sometimes with scanty grass and other nest materials of local origin.

EGGS AND YOUNG. *Eggs:* 2; ground-colour various shades of olive, brown, yellow and green, spotted and blotched dark brown; incubation 25–26 days. *Chick:* Covered with brown down, the shade varying individually; leaves nest within a few hours. Ring number 3.

SEASON. Late May to mid-July.

WIGEON *Anas penelope* Plate 17   Duck Family
PGBB, p. 151, plates 48, 50, 90, 91

HABITAT AND RANGE. Lochs and lochans in moorland districts, and dry rough grazings and hillsides, also locally on coastal marshes. Resident, breeding in many parts of Scotland N of the Forth–Clyde line, also more locally S to Border, in Cumberland, and occasionally E coast counties S to Kent; has bred inland in Thames valley in recent years.

NEST. Always on ground among heather or other vegetation, lined with grass and similar local materials, down (dark but paler at centre and tips) and feathers (white, sometimes with grey centres). Eggs covered with down in bird's absence.

EGGS AND YOUNG. *Eggs:* 7–8; elliptical, cream or buff; incubation by duck only, 24–25 days. *Duckling:* Various shades of

117

buff marbled various shades of brown; leaves nest soon after birth, when whole brood hatched. Ring number 3, but must not be ringed till fairly well feathered.

SEASON. May and June.

COMMON POCHARD *Aythya ferina* Plate 23
PGBB, p. 152, plates 48, 52, 89, 93   [Duck Family

HABITAT AND RANGE. Freshwater lakes, lochs and ponds surrounded by fairly thick vegetation. Resident, breeding locally in many parts of Scotland, E and S England and Anglesey; has bred Ireland.

NEST. On ground in thick aquatic vegetation, much closer to water than most ducks. Similar to coot's; made of sedges and similar local materials, but lined with down (brown with pale centres) and feathers. Eggs covered with down in bird's absence.

EGGS AND YOUNG. *Eggs:* 6–11; elliptical, greenish-grey; incubation by duck only, about 25 days. *Duckling:* Covered with yellowish down marbled blackish-brown; leaves nest after a few hours. Ring number 3, but must not be ringed till fairly well feathered.

SEASON. Late April to mid-June.

GOLDENEYE (*Bucephala clangula*), Plate 45; Duck Family (*PGBB*, p. 152, plates 47, 51, 88, 91, 93). Said to have bred Cheshire 1931–32, in rabbit burrows; suspected of having bred occasionally in Scotland, but never proved. Normally nest always in hole in tree, sometimes at height of 50 feet or more; uses nest-boxes abroad. Eggs bluish-green.

FULMAR *Fulmarus glacialis* Plate 41   Shearwater Family
PGBB, p. 153, plates 61, 101, 104, 107

HABITAT AND RANGE. Sea-cliffs throughout the British Isles, except between Norfolk and Devon, and prospecting many places even there.

NEST. Colonial; almost always on a ledge on a sea-cliff, or on flat top of cliff or stack, very exceptionally on a building or a crag a few miles inland, or in a shallow burrow. No nest material, except sometimes small pebbles.

118

EGGS AND YOUNG. *Eggs:* 1; matt white; incubation period unusually variable but averaging 53 days. *Nestling:* Covered with white and pale blue-grey down; fledging period also very variable, averaging 46 days. Ring number 3.

SEASON. Early May to mid-September.

GREAT CRESTED GREBE *Podiceps cristatus* Plate 27

PGBB, p. 153, plates 47, 99, 110, 111   [Grebe Family

HABITAT AND RANGE. Inland waters, usually more than 5 acres in extent and with plenty of cover, including slow-flowing rivers. Resident, scattered throughout England and Ireland, and locally in Scotland and Wales, not in Isle of Man.

NEST. Always surrounded by water but not often far from some kind of cover; may be floating and anchored or grounded on some obstruction or vegetation. A pile of waterweed, eggs covered over when bird away.

EGGS AND YOUNG. *Eggs:* 3–4; elliptical, matt white when fresh but soon discoloured by wet waterweeds or iron-stained water; incubation about 28 days. *Chick:* Covered with blackish and buffish down, and having a very striped appearance, especially on head and neck; utters a very characteristic high-pitched piping food-call. Ring number Clip 4, but must not be ringed till fairly well feathered.

SEASON. April to July or August; sometimes two broods.

SCAUP (*Aythya marila*), Plate 45; Duck Family (*PGBB*

p. 154, plates 51, 88, 92, 93). Bred several times Outer Hebrides, 1897–1913, also Sutherland 1899, Caithness 1939, W Ross 1946, probably Lincolnshire 1944, and perhaps also Orkney and elsewhere. Nest always on ground with or without cover, usually near water and often on island in loch; down dark sooty brown, feathers whitish; eggs olive matt.

COMMON SCOTER *Melanitta nigra* Plate 23

PGBB, p. 155, plates 51, 87, 89   Duck Family

HABITAT AND RANGE. Loch-studded moorland in Scotland N from Inverness, and in Islay, very local; Lough Erne in Ireland.

NEST. Always in a hollow on ground, usually close to water, sometimes on an island, generally well hidden in heather, etc. Lined with moss and similar local materials mixed with down (dark brown, pale centres) and feathers (grey, paler at tip). Eggs covered with down in bird's absence.

EGGS AND YOUNG. *Eggs:* 5–7; elliptical, cream or buff; incubation by duck only, 27–28 days. *Duckling:* Covered with blackish-brown down on upper parts, greyish-white on under parts; leaves nest soon after hatching. Ring number Clip 4, but must not be ringed till fairly well feathered.

SEASON. Late May to early July.

CAROLINA DUCK (*Aix sponsa*); Duck Family (*PGBB*, p. 156, plates 52, 54). Breeding full-winged in Bedfordshire (Woburn), Surrey (Cobham) and Gloucestershire (Slimbridge), and perhaps elsewhere. Nesting arrangements similar to mandarin duck (page 116), but eggs whiter.

GADWALL *Anas strepera* Plate 23 Duck Family
PGBB, p. 156, plates 50, 52, 91

HABITAT AND RANGE. Inland waters, such as lochs, lakes, meres, reservoirs, and slow-flowing rivers. Resident, breeding in several parts of Scotland, mainly in N and Forth area; in England several colonies of introduced birds, Cumberland, Breckland, Surrey, Gloucestershire; has bred Ireland.

NEST. Always on the ground and nearly always in thick vegetation close to water. Made of sedges and similar local materials, lined with down (dark with small pale centres and characteristic greyish-white extreme tips) and feathers (white, usually with dark centre and tip). Eggs covered with down in bird's absence.

EGGS AND YOUNG. *Eggs:* 8–12; elliptical, pale yellowish-buff, rather similar to wigeon's; incubation by duck only, 27–28 days. *Duckling:* Similar to mallard but smaller and with yellow more extensive; leaves nest as soon as whole brood hatched and dried off, can swim at once. Ring number 3, but must not be ringed until fairly well feathered.

SEASON. May and June.

SHOVELER   *Spatula clypeata*   Plate 17   Duck Family
  PGBB, p. 156, plates 50, 53, 90, 94

HABITAT AND RANGE. Neighbourhood of inland and coastal
  fresh waters with plenty of cover and shallow muddy water
  nearby. Resident, but local throughout British Isles.

NEST. Usually concealed in a hollow on fairly dry ground,
  often some distance from water on gorsy or brackeny heath-
  land, very often in a grassy meadow. Made of dried grass
  and similar local materials, lined with down (brown with
  pale centres, like both wigeon's and pintail's) and feathers
  (brown marbled black or white); grass-stems sometimes
  tented overhead. Eggs covered with down in bird's absence.

EGGS AND YOUNG. *Eggs:* 8–12; elliptical, buff, usually tinted
  green; incubation by duck only, about 24 days. *Duckling:*
  Similar to mallard; leaves nest soon after hatching. Ring
  number 4 overlapped, but must not be ringed till fairly well
  feathered.

SEASON. April to early June.

CAROLINA DUCK AT NEST-HOLE

121

WATER BIRDS: Long

LESSER BLACK-BACK *Larus fuscus* Plate 19 Gull Family
PGBB, p. 158, plates 63, 64, 108, 109

HABITAT AND RANGE. Sea-cliffs, marine islands, shingle and sand-dunes, sometimes inland on lochs and bogs. Summer visitor, widespread on coasts and inland in N England, Wales, Scotland and Ireland; also on S and SW coasts England, sparsely from Dungeness to S Devon, more commonly thence to Bristol Channel.

NEST. Colonial; either on ground or on cliff ledge or flat top of cliff or stack. Made of various local vegetable materials.

EGGS AND YOUNG. *Eggs:* 3; very similar to herring-gull's (below); incubation about 27 days. *Nestling:* Indistinguishable from herring-gull, and young birds must not be ringed in mixed colonies of the two species; fledging about 32 days, but leaves nests on flat sites some days before able to fly. Ring number 4, but must not be ringed till fairly well feathered.

SEASON. May to July; one brood only, but repeat clutches common at gulleries where eggs collected for food.

HERRING-GULL *Larus argentatus* Plate 41 Gull Family
PGBB, p. 160, plates 61, 62, 63, 101, 104, 107, 108

HABITAT AND RANGE. Sea-cliffs, rocky coasts and marine islands, also less frequently on sand-dunes and shingle, and less frequently still inland by lochs, and on bogs. Resident, breeding on cliffs throughout British Isles, except the low ones between Humber and Thames; also occasionally inland in Scotland and Ireland.

NEST. Colonial; almost always on ground or cliff-ledge, but exceptionally on a building. Made of various local vegetable materials.

EGGS AND YOUNG. *Eggs:* 3; ground-colour variable, pale blue-green, olive, buff or various shades of brown, blotched and spotted with darker brown; not certainly distinguishable

from lesser black-back's; incubation about 26 days. *Nestling:*
Covered with greyish-buff down marbled blackish-brown,
and indistinguishable from lesser black-back; fledging about
42 days, but leaves nests on flat sites some days before this.
Ring number 4, but must not be ringed till fairly well
feathered, and never in mixed colonies with lesser black-back.
SEASON. Late April to July; one brood only, but many late
clutches presumably repeats due to persistent thieving of
eggs by other gulls, and human beings.

KING-EIDER (*Somateria spectabilis*); Duck Family (*PGBB*,
p. 161–2). Scarce winter visitor to N Scotland, but probably
often overlooked owing to similarity of duck to duck
common eider; occasionally in summer, and has at least
twice been suspected of breeding, but this seems less likely
than with some other northern duck and waders, for its
nearest known breeding place is Spitsbergen. Nest normally
on ground near freshwater pool; down darker than common
eider's; eggs browner and less green than common eider's.

VELVET-SCOTER (*Melanitta fusca*), Plate 48; Duck Family
(*PGBB*, p. 161, plates 51, 87, 91). Occasionally summers in
Scottish waters and has more than once been suspected of
breeding in the northern isles, but never proved to do so.
Nest always on ground but not necessarily very close to
water; down similar to common scoter but larger; eggs
cream-coloured or buff.

RED-CRESTED POCHARD (*Netta rufina*), Plate 45; Duck
Family. (*PGBB*, p. 162, plates 48, 52). Bred in Lincolnshire in 1937, probably escapes from Woburn, where young
were reared annually and not pinioned; escapes also bred
Essex, 1958; is, however, spreading naturally on Continent
and now breeds Holland and Denmark, so that a natural
colonisation from across the North Sea is a possibility to
be reckoned with. Nest always on ground and usually near
water, and often so deeply hidden in vegetation as to appear
in a tunnel; eggs vary from pale stone-brown to pale green.

PINTAIL *Anas acuta* Plate 23   Duck Family
PGBB, p. 163, plates 50, 52, 90, 94

HABITAT AND RANGE. Inland waters in moorland districts, and
locally on coastal marshes and dunes. Resident, local in
Scotland, chiefly N of Forth–Clyde line; also in NE Ireland
and occasionally in England S to Kent.

NEST. Social. Always in a hollow in the ground, often near
water but not necessarily so; tends to be less well concealed
than most ducks' nests. Made of grasses and similar local
materials mixed with down and feathers which are both
rather similar to shoveler's. Eggs covered with down in
bird's absence.

EGGS AND YOUNG. *Eggs:* 7–9; elliptical, various shades of
yellowish (shoveler's eggs usually tinged green); incubation
by duck only, about 23 days. *Duckling:* Similar to mallard;
leaves nest soon after hatching. Ring number 3, but must
not be ringed till fairly well feathered.

SEASON. May to June.

RED-THROATED DIVER *Colymbus stellatus* Plate 24
PGBB, p. 163, plates 46, 110, 111   [Diver Family

HABITAT AND RANGE. Moorland studded with small tarns or
dubh-lochs in many parts of the Scottish Highlands and
islands as far S as Argyll, and in one locality in Donegal.

NEST. Eggs are always laid on ground or on heap of waterweeds within a foot or two of water, with a characteristic
slipway leading up to it; in a dry season, however, the water
may recede and leave the nest several yards from the edge
of the loch by hatching time.

EGGS AND YOUNG. *Eggs:* 2; olive tinted green, brown or yellow
and rather scantily spotted with dark brown; incubation
mostly by female, 26–27 days. *Chick:* Thickly covered with
mouse-brown down, and not distinguishable from black-
throated diver; leaves nest soon after hatching.

SEASON. Late May to early July.

MALLARD *Anas platyrhyncha* Plates 19, 36 Duck Family
PGBB, p. 164, plates 50, 53, 90, 94

HABITAT AND RANGE. Near almost any kind of fresh water, including lakes in town parks, and by sea-lochs. Resident, common throughout British Isles.

NEST. Site very variable, often on ground in thick herbage, under bramble brakes, in alder-holt or tuft of sedge; also not infrequently in hollow in tree or tree-stump, especially pollard willow; occasionally in old nest of other bird or on building. Made of dried grasses and similar local materials, mixed with down (brown with pale centres and tips) and characteristic feathers (whitish with brown patches). Eggs covered by down when bird absent.

EGGS AND YOUNG. *Eggs:* 8–10; elliptical, greenish tinged buff or grey; incubation by duck only, about 28 days. *Duckling:* Covered with yellowish-buff down marbled blackish-brown; leaves nest as soon as whole brood hatched and dried off. Ring number 4, but must not be ringed till fairly well feathered.

BREEDING SEASON. Mid-March to May, but owing to artificial conditions in which many estate-bred mallard live nests may be found in almost any month of year; occasional second broods are also probably due to artificial conditions.

EIDER *Somateria mollissima* Plate 26   Duck Family
PGBB, p. 165, plates 50, 51, 87, 88, 89, 92

HABITAT AND RANGE. Rocky and sandy sea-coasts, and marine islands, where there are grassy slopes. Resident on all coasts of Scotland and isles, except from Caithness to Rattray Head (Aberdeenshire), and somewhat local both thence S to Coquet Island (Northumberland) with historic and important colony on Farne Islands, and in SW Scotland; has bred Walney Island (Lancashire); in Ireland appears to be extending its range from Donegal.

NEST. Social; always on ground on sand, shingle, rocky ledges or moorland near the sea; either with or without cover. Nest made of grass and similar local materials (exceptionally of freak materials such as wood shavings), usually well lined with down (pale grey-brown, paler in middle and at tips) and characteristic feather (brown barred black). Eggs covered with down when bird absent.

EGGS AND YOUNG. *Eggs:* 4–5; elliptical, green, usually tinted olive or grey, or buff, often with stain spots; incubation by duck only, 27–28 days. *Ducklings:* Covered with blackish-brown down; leaves nest as soon as whole brood hatched and dried off. Ring number Clip 4, but must not be ringed till fairly well feathered.

SEASON. May to early July.

RED-BREASTED MERGANSER *Mergus serrator* Plates 8, 20. *PGBB*, p. 166, plates 46, 48, 53, 91, 94 [Duck Family

HABITAT AND RANGE. Rivers, lochs and low-lying coastal areas in most Scottish coastal counties (but not S of Aberdeen on E side) and in many parts of Ireland, especially in N and W. Has bred in Anglesey.

NEST. Always either on, or in cavity in, ground, usually under cover of thick vegetation, boulders, or tree roots. Made of grass and similar local materials, lined with down (darker than goosander's, with pale centres and tips) and smaller whitish feathers than goosander. Eggs covered with down when bird absent.

EGGS AND YOUNG. *Eggs:* 7–12; elliptical, stone-coloured or buffish, sometimes with a greenish tinge; incubation by duck only, about 29 days. *Duckling:* Similar to goosander (below); leaves nest soon after hatching. Ring number 4 overlapped, but must not be ringed till fairly well feathered.

SEASON. Late May to early July.

GREAT SKUA *Stercorarius skua* Plate 26   Skua Family
PGBB, p. 167, plates 63, 106

HABITAT AND RANGE. Barren moorlands near the sea in Orkney, Shetland and the Outer Hebrides; has bred on mainland; summer visitor.

NEST. Social; always on the ground; sparsely lined with lichen and similar local materials.

EGGS AND YOUNG. *Eggs:* 2; ground-colour various shades of cream, brown, gold, olive and green; spotted and blotched

WATER BIRDS: LONG

with dark brown or blackish; incubation 29–30 days. *Nestling:* Covered with brown down tinted yellowish, pinkish and greyish; fledging about 46 days, but young birds wander away from nest soon after hatching. Ring number 4.

SEASON. May to July.

SHELD-DUCK *Tadorna tadorna* Plate 2   Duck Family
PGBB, p. 167, plates 55, 56, 94, 96

HABITAT AND RANGE. Sand-dunes, sandy and muddy coasts and estuaries; also occasionally rough heathy places and exceptionally even woods and farmland, but very rarely more than a mile or two from salt water, except in the Fens. Resident on all suitable coasts of British Isles.

NEST. Usually in a borrow or hole in the ground, but sometimes under cover of boulders, bushes or other thick vegetation, and in one of two localities regularly in holes in trees. Nest of very scanty grasses and similar local materials with plenty of down (uniform pale brownish-grey) and feathers (white, tipped dark brown or chestnut). Eggs covered with down when bird absent.

EGGS AND YOUNG. *Eggs:* 8–15; elliptical, creamy-white; incubation by duck only, about 28 days. *Duckling:* Covered with white down, marbled with various shades of brown on upper parts; leaves nest shortly after whole brood are hatched. Ring number 4, but must not be ringed till fairly well feathered.

SEASON. May and June.

BLACK-THROATED DIVER *Colymbus arcticus* Plate 24
PGBB, p. 168, plates 96, 110   [Diver Family

HABITAT AND RANGE. Larger inland lochs in many parts of W and Central Scottish Highlands and Outer Hebrides.

NEST. Eggs almost always laid on ground (exceptionally on a heap of waterweeds) within a foot or two of water, with a characteristic slipway leading up to it; usually on an island or islet, but sometimes on main shore of loch, usually on a promontory.

EGGS AND YOUNG. *Eggs:* 2; olive or brown, rather sparsely

127

spotted, blotched and streaked with black, larger than red-throated diver's; incubation about 29 days. *Chick:* Thickly covered with mouse-brown down and only distinguishable from red-throated diver by size; leaves nest soon after hatching. Ring size 19 mm.

SEASON. May and June.

GOOSANDER *Mergus merganser* Plate 6   Duck Family
PGBB, p. 169, plates 48, 53, 91, 94

HABITAT AND RANGE. Lochs and rivers over a wide area of the Scottish Highlands, more locally in the lowlands, and has recently spread into Northumberland.

NEST. Usually in a hole in a tree, but also in cavity in bank or pile of boulders. Nest material of rotten wood only in trees, but dried grass and similar local materials in other holes, lined with pale grey down and white feathers, with which eggs are covered in bird's absence.

EGGS AND YOUNG. *Eggs:* 7–13; elliptical, creamy-white; incubation by duck only, 34–35 days. *Duckling:* Covered with grey-brown down marbled tawny and white; not distinguishable from red-breasted merganser in the field; leaves nest after 2–3 days. Ring number 4, but must not be ringed until fairly well feathered.

SEASON. Mid-April to early June.

GREAT BLACK-BACK *Larus marinus* Plate 19   Gull Family
PGBB, p. 170, plates 63, 64, 96, 108, 109

HABITAT AND RANGER. Sea cliffs and rocky marine islands, sometimes also inland moors and island in freshwater loughs. Resident, widespread on coasts and island of Scotland (not S of Moray Firth on E side), Ireland (chiefly in W), Wales and SW England (Dorset to Bristol Channel); also inland in NW England and NW Ireland.

NEST. Social; always on ground or top of rocky stack or cliff ledge, very often on rocky outcrop or promontory on cliff or island. Nest a fairly substantial affair of heather, seaweed and other local materials.

EGGS AND YOUNG. *Eggs:* 3; usually buff or olive-brown, but occasionally bluish, blotched and spotted with dark brown; incubation about 27 days. *Nestling:* Larger than, but otherwise hardly distinguishable from herring-gull, but tends to be somewhat paler and greyer; leaves nest after two or three weeks and wanders off into thick vegetation until it can fly. Ring number Clip 4.

SEASON. May to July.

GREAT BLACK-BACK CHICK

WATER BIRDS: Very Long

EGYPTIAN GOOSE (*Alopochen aegyptiacus*), Plate 36; Duck
Family (*PGBB*, p. 172, plate 55). Full-winged breeding
colonies are acclimatised in N Norfolk and elsewhere in
England, and a pair bred in Hertfordshire in 1938. Nest
usually in a cavity in a tree, but sometimes in old nest of
other bird, in a burrow or on the ground. Eggs yellowish-
white, hatching in January or February.

GREAT NORTHERN DIVER (*Colymbus immer*), Plate 48;
Diver Family (*PGBB*, p. 172, plates 96, 110, 111). Often
summers in Scottish isles, and has probably bred more than
once, especially in Shetland, but this has never been proved.
Eggs and nesting arrangements resemble those of red-
throated and black-throated divers.

SHAG *Phalacrocorax aristotelis* Plate 42 Cormorant Family
PGBB, p. 173, plates 64, 96, 110, 111
HABITAT AND RANGE. Rocky and cliff-bound coasts through-
out Scotland (local on E coast), Ireland (local on E coast) and
Wales; in England only on Farne Islands (Northumberland),
St. Bees Head (Cumberland), and from Isle of Wight to
Lundy (Bristol Channel). Never inland.
NEST. Colonial; sometimes adjacent to cormorants, but rarely
mixing with them; almost always on rock or cliff ledges, but
occasionally among boulders. Made of tough sticks, stems
and seaweed stipes, lined mainly with grass.
EGGS AND YOUNG. *Eggs:* 3; elliptical, like comorant's (p. 131)
but smaller; incubation 30–35 days. *Nestling:* No down
at birth but soon acquires thick covering of brown down
paler than cormorant; leaves nest at about 53 days. Ring
size 19 mm., but must not be ringed till fairly well feathered.
SEASON. April to July; perhaps sometimes two broods.

GREAT AUK (*Alca impennis*), p. 154, Auk Family. Extinct since 1844; formerly bred on St. Kilda (Outer Hebrides) and probably also on Orkney and elsewhere. Was colonial, breeding on rock ledges on marine islands. Egg pear-shaped and resembling large common guillemot's.

CORMORANT *Phalacrocorax carbo* Plates 26, 42
PGBB, p. 173, plates 64, 96, 110, 111 [Cormorant Family
HABITAT AND RANGE. Cliff-bound coasts and rocky marine islands, also exceptionally inland, usually near fresh water. Resident, breeding round most coasts of British Isles, but local or absent on E coasts both Great Britain and Ireland.
NEST. Colonial, sometimes adjacent to shags but rarely mixing with them; usually on rock or cliff ledge, but occasionally in trees inland. Made of seaweed on coast, but of various local materials inland.
EGGS AND YOUNG. *Eggs:* 3–4; elliptical, pale blue, but so covered with thick chalky deposit that true colour shows through only in patches or not at all; stains very readily; incubation about 35 days. *Nestling:* No down at first but soon covered with thick dark brown down, darker than shag; leaves nest at about 7 weeks. Ring size 19 mm. but must not be ringed till fairly well feathered.
SEASON. April to early August; perhaps sometimes two broods.

GANNET *Sula bassana* Plates 26, 41   Booby Family
PGBB, p. 174, plates 58, 86, 109, 110, 112
HABITAT AND RANGE. Sea-cliffs and rocky marine islands, mainly on N and W coasts British Isles. Largest colonies on St. Kilda and Sula Sgeir (Outer Hebrides), Sule Stack (Orkney), Hermaness and Noss (Shetland), Bass Rock (Firth of Forth), Ailsa Craig (Ayrshire), Grassholm (Pembrokeshire), Little Skellig and Bull Rock (SW Ireland); a few small colonies elsewhere, but none on mainland Great Britain or Ireland, except at Bempton (Yorkshire).
NEST. Colonial; always on cliff or rock ledge; made of seaweed and other local materials.

EGGS AND YOUNG. *Eggs:* 1; elliptical, like cormorant has blue egg, heavily overlaid with chalky white deposit and readily staining; incubation about 44 days. *Nestling:* At first very sparsely covered with whitish down, later thickly covered with white down; leaves nest at 9–10 weeks. Ring size 16 mm.

SEASON. April to August.

YOUNG GANNET

WATER BIRDS: Huge

CANADA GOOSE *Branta canadensis* Plate 24 Duck Family
PGBB, p. 175, plates 56, 95, 96

HABITAT AND RANGE. Freshwater lakes, meres and ponds.
Resident (introduced) in many parts of England, especially
Home Counties, E Anglia, Northants, and the W Midlands
N to Cheshire; scarce in N and SW England and in Wales;
in Scotland only in Tay, Forth and Moray areas.

NEST. Social; nest always on ground close to water, fairly well
hidden in vegetation, often on an island. Made of dried
grass, sedge and similar local materials, mixed with down
(greyish-brown with white centre and pale tip), and whitish
feathers. Eggs covered with down when bird absent.

EGGS AND YOUNG. *Eggs:* 5–6; elliptical, dirty white, matt;
incubation by goose only, 28–29 days. *Gosling:* Covered
with greenish-brown and greenish-yellow down; leaves nest
shortly after hatching. Ring size 19 mm.

SEASON. April and May.

WHOOPER SWAN (*Cygnus cygnus*), Plate 24; Duck Family
(*PGBB*, p. 176, plates 58, 86). A few pairs bred in Scotland,
mainly in Central Highlands, during 1919–39, and a pair
attempted to breed in 1944, but though a few still stay the
summer, there have been no definite breeding records in
recent years. Huge nest like mute swan in marsh or close
to fresh water, often on island. Eggs creamy-white, staining
readily.

MUTE SWAN *Cygnus olor* Plate 24   Duck Family
PGBB, p. 177, plates 58, 86

HABITAT AND RANGE. All kinds of fresh water, swamps, rivers,
canals, ponds, flooded gravel-pits, lakes, reservoirs, also sea
lochs; common in town parks. Resident (semi-domesticated)
almost throughout British Isles. Colonial only at Abbots-
bury (Dorset).

NEST. A huge pile of sedges, waterweeds and similar local materials in a swamp or close to water; often on an island.

EGGS AND YOUNG. *Eggs:* 5–7; elliptical, white tinged grey or blue-green; incubation chiefly by pen (female), about 35 days. *Cygnet:* Covered with down, grey-brown above and whitish below; leaves nest shortly after hatching. Ring size M.

SEASON. April to June.

PAIR OF MUTE SWANS AND VERY YOUNG CYGNETS

THE KEY

THE KEY is arranged in seven main sections:

Colonial and Social Nesting (p. 137).

Nest Sites (p. 138).

Nest Construction (p. 143).

Nest Materials (p. 144).

Egg Shape (p. 146).

Egg Colour (p. 148).

Nestlings (p. 152).

As in *The Pocket Guide to British Birds*, the names of the birds are printed in three types, viz.: ordinary type for land birds, *italics* for waterside birds, and SMALL CAPITAL LETTERS for water birds. For definitions of these habitat groupings, see p. 10 of the Introduction.

Within each subsection, the birds are divided into eight size-groupings based on length, as described and defined on p. 11. The groups are abbreviated as follows:

VS	Very Short	**ML**	Medium Long
S	Short	**L**	Long
MS	Medium Short	**VL**	Very Long
M	Medium	**H**	Huge

Other abbreviations used in the key are:

esp especially   occ occasional

HOW TO USE THE KEY

AS WITH THE KEY to *The Pocket Guide to British Birds*, which is based on similar principles, the present Key is not intended to be exhaustive. It is meant to help you by picking out certain salient characteristics that may strike you when coming across a nest of eggs or young birds that is strange to you. It is therefore arranged in list form, and the same bird may occur in several lists.

Let us suppose, for instance, that *in a bush in your garden you find a mud-lined nest containing blue eggs with black spots*. Here are three clues that can be followed up in the Key. First, look under **Nest Sites (bushes and low trees)**, then under **Nest Materials (nest lined with mud)**, and finally under **Egg Colour (blue, marked)**. The only bird appearing under all three is the *song-thrush*. But that is an easy one, for the song-thrush is one of the very few British breeding birds that lines its nest with a mixture of mud and vegetable fibres or chips with no softer lining of grass or hair or feathers. For another example, let us suppose that you have found, *on the shingle of a south-coast beach, four pear-shaped eggs that are buff-coloured with blackish spots*. This time reference to **Nest Sites (ground)**, **Egg Shape (pear-shaped)** and **Egg Colour (buff marked)** will yield several possibilities, and it will be necessary to consult the main text to discover that the *ringed plover* is the most likely owner of the nest. To make absolutely sure, you may have to retire a short distance and watch the bird return to the nest.

In short, the Key endeavours to make the most of whatever distinctive features a nest or its contents may have, but since nests, eggs, and nestlings generally speaking, are less distinctive that the adult birds, the present Key is bound to be less helpful than that in *The Pocket Guide to British Birds*. As already indicated in the Introduction, often the only sure way of identifying many nests is to wait till one of the parent birds returns to it.

The Key covers all the birds for which full details are given in the main text, but omits the casual breeders or those which have been suspected of breeding but never proved to do so.

COLONIAL AND SOCIAL NESTING

THE MAJORITY of British birds breed in isolation, and indeed drive all others of their own species away from their territories with some vigour. A list of the solitary breeding species would therefore be of little value, but the two following lists of birds which breed either in colonies or in loose social aggregations may be of some help. Of course, you may sometimes find isolated nests of any colonial or social bird, and some, such as the dabchick, are perhaps more often solitary than social.

Colonial Breeders (nests or nest-holes close together): **VS:** House-martin, *sand-martin, reed-warbler*; **S:** Tree-sparrow, house-sparrow, swift; **M:** Jackdaw, London pigeon, rook, *lit tern, rock-dove, com tern, arctic tern, roseate tern,* MANX SHEARWATER, PUFFIN, B/N GREBE, B/H GULL; **ML:** *Sandwich tern, avocet,* COM GULL, KITTIWAKE, GUILLEMOT, FULMAR; **L:** LESSER BLACK-BACK, HERRING-GULL; **VL:** *Heron,* SHAG, CORMORANT, GANNET; **H:** MUTE SWAN (Dorset only).

Social Breeders (nests or nest-holes more loosely aggregated than above, but still fairly close together): **VS:** Redpoll, *marsh-warbler, sedge-warbler*; **S:** Linnet, twite, greenfinch, crossbill, hawfinch, STORM-PETREL, R/N PHALAROPE; **MS:** Swallow, *dunlin,* F/T PETREL; **M:** *Stock-dove,* DABCHICK, B/N GREBE, SLAVONIAN GREBE, BLACK GUILLEMOT; **ML:** Chough, Montagu's harrier, COOT, RAZORBILL, ARCTIC SKUA, G/C GREBE; **L:** PINTAIL, EIDER, GT SKUA, GT BLACK-BACK; (N.B.—Many Ducks and Geese nest in close proximity to each other when resorting to small islands.)

NEST SITES

ONLY VERY BROAD groupings are given here, and generally speaking the most typical nest sites for the birds in question. Freak nest sites cannot be allowed for in such a key as this.

Banks: VS: Wren, willow-warbler, coal-tit (hole), blue tit (hole, occ), whinchat, stonechat, *sand-martin* (hole); **S:** Twite, com redstart, robin, meadow-pipit (occ), tree-pipit, yellowhammer, cirl-bunting (occ), wryneck (hole, occ), *rock-pipit, kingfisher* (hole); **MS:** Pied wagtail, song-thrush (occ), *grey wagtail*; **M:** Ring-ouzel, blackbird, mistle-thrush (occ), stock-dove (occ); **ML:** Hooded crow (occ); **L:** Raven (steep, occ), R/B MERGANSER (occ), GOOSANDER (occ).

Buildings: VS: House-martin, *sand-martin* (occ, hole); **S:** Spotted flycatcher, com redstart (occ), black redstart, robin, chaffinch (occ), swift; **MS:** Pied wagtail, swallow, starling, lit owl, song-thrush (occ), *grey wagtail, dipper* (bridges); **M:** Ring-ouzel (occ, derelict), blackbird (occ), mistle-thrush (occ), jackdaw, stock-dove, London pigeon, kestrel, barn-owl, B/H GULL (occ); **ML:** Tawny owl (occ), peregrine (occ), woodpigeon (occ), rook (occ), carrion-crow (occ), KITTI-WAKE (occ), FULMAR (occ); **VL:** HERRING-GULL (occ), MALLARD (occ).

Bushes and Low Trees: VS: Goldcrest (occ), wren, willow-warbler (occ), chiffchaff, goldfinch, redpoll, grasshopper-warbler (occ, low bush), Dartford warbler, stonechat (gorse), *reed-warbler, marsh-warbler* (occ), *sedge-warbler*; **S:** Linnet, twite, lesser whitethroat, com whitethroat, garden-warbler, blackcap, l/t tit, house-sparrow (occ), greenfinch, bullfinch, chaffinch, hedge-sparrow, cirl-bunting, yellowhammer, nightingale (occ), r/b shrike; **MS:** Corn-bunting (occ), song-thrush, blackbird, mistle-thrush (occ), turtle-dove, sparrow-hawk (occ), jay, MOORHEN, B/H GULL (occ); **ML:** Woodpigeon,

magpie, rook (occ), carrion-crow (occ), hooded crow (occ);
VL: *Heron* (occ).

Cliffs, Crags and Quarries: VS: House-martin, *sand-martin*
(occ); **S:** Spotted flycatcher (occ), com redstart (occ), black
redstart (occ), tree-sparrow (occ), swift (occ), *rock-pipit*;
MS: Swallow (occ, caves), starling, lit owl (occ), *grey wagtail*
(occ, by rivers), *dipper* (by rivers); **M:** Ring-ouzel (occ),
mistle-thrush (occ), merlin (occ), jackdaw, stock-dove,
London pigeon, kestrel, barn-owl, *rock-dove*, BLACK GUILLE-
MOT; **ML:** Tawny owl (occ), chough, peregrine, carrion-
crow, hooded crow, com buzzard, COM GULL (occ), KITTIWAKE,
RAZORBILL, GUILLEMOT, FULMAR; **L:** Raven, LESSER BLACK-
BACK, HERRING-GULL, GOOSANDER (occ), GT BLACK-BACK;
VL: Golden eagle, *heron* (Wales), SHAG, CORMORANT, GANNET.

Creeper on Trees and Walls: VS: Goldcrest (occ), wren, willow-
warbler (occ), chiffchaff (occ), tree-creeper; **S:** Linnet (occ),
spotted flycatcher, robin, house-sparrow, greenfinch, bullfinch, chaffinch, hedge-sparrow, cirl-bunting (occ), yellowhammer (occ); **MS:** Pied wagtail (occ), song-thrush, *grey
wagtail* (walls by rivers), *dipper* (by rivers); **M:** Blackbird;
ML: Woodpigeon (trees).

Ground (on the): **VS:** Willow-warbler, wood-warbler, grasshopper-warbler, whinchat, stonechat; **S:** Twite, com redstart, robin, meadow-pipit, tree-pipit, wood-lark, cirl-bunting
(occ), yellowhammer, nightingale, *reed-bunting, l/r plover,
Kentish plover, rock-pipit, yellow wagtail*, R/N PHALAROPE;
MS: Corn-bunting, skylark, quail, dotterel, song-thrush
(occ), *dunlin, ringed plover, com sandpiper, spotted crake*;
M: Ring-ouzel, blackbird (occ), nightjar, corncrake, golden
plover, merlin, lapwing, com partridge, stock-dove (occ),
kestrel (occ), l/e owl, woodcock, ptarmigan, red grouse, r/l
partridge, *lit tern, com snipe, water-rail, com redshank*, greenshank, com tern, arctic tern, roseate tern, TEAL, B/H GULL;
ML: S/e owl, tawny owl (occ), peregrine (occ), woodpigeon

(Orkney), black grouse, Montagu's harrier, hen-harrier, hooded crow (occ), com buzzard (occ), *whimbrel, bl/t godwit, Sandwich tern, avocet, oystercatcher, marsh-harrier*, GAR- GANEY, COM GULL, TUFTED DUCK, ARCTIC SKUA, WIGEON, COM POCHARD, COM SCOTER, GADWALL, SHOVELER; **L:** Pheasant, capercaillie, *curlew*, LESSER BLACK-BACK, HERRING-GULL, PIN- TAIL, R/T DIVER, MALLARD, EIDER, R/B MERGANSER, GT SKUA, SHELD-DUCK (occ), B/T DIVER, GT BLACK-BACK; **VL:** Golden eagle (occ), *g/l goose, bittern, heron* (occ), CORMORANT (rocks), GANNET (rocks); **H:** CANADA GOOSE, MUTE SWAN.

Herbage (i.e. long grass, heather, nettles, etc.): **VS:** Willow- warbler (occ), chiffchaff, grasshopper-warbler, Dartford warbler (heather), *reed-warbler* (esp reeds), *marsh-warbler* (esp nettles), *sedge-warbler*; **S:** Linnet, twite, com white- throat, garden-warbler, blackcap (occ), bullfinch (occ, heather), hedge-sparrow, nightingale, *reed-bunting, bearded tit* (reeds, sedge); **MS:** Corn-bunting (occ); **M:** Ring-ouzel (occ, heather); **ML:** Magpie (occ, heather).

Hole in Ground: VS: Coal-tit, crested tit (occ); **S:** Com red- start (occ), gt tit (occ), wheatear, snow-bunting (among stones), STORM-PETREL; **MS:** Pied wagtail, lit owl, F/T PETREL; **M:** Jackdaw (occ), stock-dove (occ), MANX SHEARWATER, PUFFIN, BLACK GUILLEMOT; **ML:** Tawny owl (occ); **L** R/B MERGANSER, SHELD-DUCK, GOOSANDER (occ).

Hole in Tree: VS: Coal-tit, crested tit, blue tit, marsh-tit, willow-tit, tree-creeper (crevice), pied flycatcher; **S:** Spotted flycatcher (hollow), com redstart, nuthatch (plastered up), gt tit, tree-sparrow, house-sparrow (occ), barred woodpecker, wryneck; **MS:** Pied wagtail (occ), starling, lit owl, pied woodpecker; **M:** Hoopoe, green woodpecker, jackdaw, stock-dove, kestrel (hollow), jay (occ, London area), barn- owl (hollow); **ML:** Tawny owl. MANDARIN DUCK; **L:** MAL- LARD (hollow), SHELD-DUCK (occ), GOOSANDER.

THE KEY

Hole in Wall: VS: Coal-tit, blue tit, marsh-tit (occ), tree-creeper (occ), pied flycatcher (occ), *sand-martin* (occ); **S:** Twite (occ), spotted flycatcher (ledge), com redstart, black redstart (ledge), robin (occ), nuthatch (occ), gt tit, tree-sparrow, house-sparrow, wheatear (occ), wryneck (occ), swift, *rock-pipit* (occ), *kingfisher* (occ), STORM-PETREL (occ); **MS:** Pied wagtail, starling, lit owl, *grey wagtail* (ledge, near water), F/T PETREL; **M:** Hoopoe (occ), jackdaw, stock-dove, London pigeon, barn-owl, BLACK GUILLEMOT (occ); **L:** SHELD-DUCK (occ).

Nest-box: VS: Wren (occ), coal-tit, blue tit, marsh-tit (occ), tree-creeper (occ), pied flycatcher; **S:** Spotted flycatcher (ledge), com redstart, robin, nuthatch (occ), gt tit, tree-sparrow, house-sparrow, wryneck (occ), swift (occ); **MS:** Pied wagtail (occ), starling, lit owl (occ), pied woodpecker (occ); **M:** Hoopoe (occ), stock-dove (occ), barn-owl, l/e owl (occ, platform); **ML:** Tawny owl (occ).

Old Nest of Other Bird: VS: Wren (occ), coal-tit (occ), blue tit (occ); **S:** Spotted flycatcher (occ), com redstart (occ), nuthatch (occ), gt tit (occ), tree-sparrow (occ), house-sparrow (esp martins'), hedge-sparrow (occ), swift (occ); **MS:** Pied wagtail (occ), starling (esp woodpeckers'), lit owl (occ), *grey wagtail* (occ), *com sandpiper* (occ); **M:** Turtle-dove (occ, uses basis), merlin (occ), sparrowhawk (occ), hobby (esp carrion-crow's), jackdaw, stock-dove, kestrel (esp carrion-crow's and magpie's), l/e owl (ditto), MOORHEN (occ); **ML:** Tawny owl (occ), peregrine, woodpigeon (uses basis), black grouse (occ), com buzzard (uses basis), COM GULL (occ); **L:** Pheasant (occ), capercaillie (occ), MALLARD (occ).

Other Birds' Nests: M: Com partridge (occ), cuckoo, r/l partridge (occ), MOORHEN (occ, coot's); **ML:** COOT (occ, moorhen's); **L:** Pheasant (occ).

Trees: VS: Goldcrest (conifer), goldfinch, siskin (conifer), redpoll; **S:** Linnet (occ), spotted flycatcher (trunk), l/t tit,

141

house-sparrow, greenfinch, bullfinch (occ), chaffinch, hedge-sparrow (occ), cirl-bunting (occ), hawfinch, crossbill (conifer), r/b shrike (occ); **MS:** Song-thrush; **M:** Golden oriole, blackbird, mistle-thrush, turtle-dove (occ), merlin (occ), sparrowhawk, hobby, jackdaw (occ), kestrel, jay, l/e owl, MOORHEN; **ML:** Woodpigeon, magpie, rook, carrion-crow, hooded crow, com buzzard; **L:** Kite, raven, MALLARD (pollards); **VL:** Golden eagle, *heron*, CORMORANT (occ).

Water (floating or islanded): **M:** DABCHICK, B/N GREBE, SLAVONIAN GREBE, MOORHEN, B/H GULL; **ML:** COOT, TUFTED DUCK (occ), COM POCHARD, G/C GREBE; **L:** R/T DIVER (occ); **VL:** *Bittern*; **H:** MUTE SWAN.

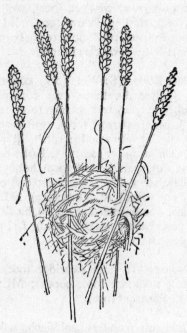

NEST OF HARVEST-MOUSE

NEST CONSTRUCTION

Domed Nests: **VS:** Wren, willow-warbler, chiffchaff, wood-warbler; **S:** L/t tit, house-sparrow; **MS:** *Dipper*; **ML:** Magpie. N.B.—Mice make loosely domed nests of grasses, etc., close to the ground.

Nests with 'Handles': **VS:** Goldcrest, *marsh-warbler*; **S:** Com whitethroat (occ), blackcap; **M:** Golden oriole.

Nests with Access by a Runway (sometimes covered): **VS:** Grasshopper-warbler, whinchat, stonechat; **S:** Meadow-pipit, tree-pipit, woodlark; **MS:** Skylark; **M:** Com partridge, r/l partridge; **ML:** COM POCHARD; **L:** R/T DIVER, R/B MERGANSER, SHELD-DUCK, B/T DIVER.

Tented Nests: **M:** Corncrake (occ), *com redshank*, MOORHEN; **ML:** TUFTED DUCK, SHOVELER.

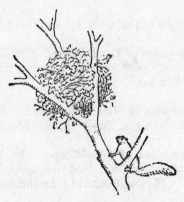

SQUIRREL'S DREY

NEST MATERIALS

THE NESTS of the majority of British breeding birds are made of dried grass or some other local vegetable material and lined with a combination of similar materials together with animal hair or animal or vegetable down, as available. The section of the key which follows applies only to nests departing from this general pattern. So many nests of ground-nesting species may or may not have nest material that there seemed little point in listing nests with no nest material.

Nest Made Largely of Bark Flakes: S: Nuthatch.

Nest Made Largely of Disgorged Fish-Bones: S: *Kingfisher*.

Nest Made Largely of Moss: VS: Goldcrest, wren, goldfinch, siskin; **S:** Spotted flycatcher, robin, l/t tit, greenfinch, chaffinch, wheatear, hedge-sparrow; **MS:** Song-thrush, *dipper*.

Nest Made Largely of Mud: VS: House-martin; **MS:** Swallow.

Nest with Foundation of Dead Leaves: VS: Chiffchaff, pied flycatcher, grasshopper-warbler; **S:** Robin, nuthatch, nightingale; **M:** Woodcock.

Nest with Foundation of Moss: VS: Coal-tit, crested tit, blue tit, marsh-tit; **S:** Gt tit, tree-pipit, wood-lark, cirl-bunting.

Nest with Foundation of Wood-Chips: VS: Willow-tit; **S:** Barred woodpecker; **MS:** Pied woodpecker; **M:** Green woodpecker. (The woodpeckers have no other nest-material.)

Nest Lined with Feathers: VS: Goldcrest, wren, willow-warbler, chiffchaff, coal-tit (occ), crested tit, blue tit, willow-tit, redpoll (occ), tree-creeper, Dartford warbler (occ),

house-martin, *sand-martin*; S: Linnet (occ), twite (occ), com
redstart, black redstart, l/t tit, tree-sparrow, house-sparrow,
greenfinch, chaffinch (occ), wheatear (occ), hedge-sparrow
(occ), crossbill, swift, r/b shrike (occ); MS: Pied wagtail
(occ), swallow, starling; M: Hoopoe (occ), com partridge
(occ), ptarmigan, red grouse.

    N.B.—All ducks and geese line their nests with a mixture
of their own feathers and down.

Nest Lined with Mud: MS: Song-thrush; **M:** Blackbird
(covered with dried grass), mistle-thrush (do.); **ML:** Magpie.

Nest Largely Made of Twigs: M: Turtle-dove, jackdaw,
London pigeon, jay; **ML:** Chough, woodpigeon, magpie,
rook, carrion-crow, hooded crow, com buzzard; **L:** Kite,
raven; **VL:** Golden eagle, *heron*.

Nest with Foundation of Twigs: VS: Redpoll; **S:** Greenfinch,
bullfinch, hedge-sparrow, crossbill, hawfinch.

Nest Lining Covering Eggs during Bird's Absence: VS: Coal-tit,
crested tit, blue tit, marsh-tit, willow-tit; **S:** Nuthatch, gt tit;
M: com. partridge, red grouse, DABCHICK, B/N GREBE,
SLAVONIAN GREBE; **ML:** G/C GREBE; **L:** Capercaillie. All
ducks and geese.

Nest Decorations:
  Spiders' Cocoons, etc., on Rim: VS: Dartford warbler; **S:**
Lesser whitethroat, com whitethroat, blackcap.
  Greenery: VS: Blue tit; **S:** Hawfinch; **MS:** Song-thrush (ivy
berries); **M:** MOORHEN; **ML:** Com buzzard; **VL:** Golden
eagle.
  Lichens: VS: Goldfinch, siskin; **S:** L/t tit, chaffinch.
  White Objects: S: Greenfinch (on rim), chaffinch (occ);
MS: Song-thrush (occ); **M:** Golden oriole, blackbird (occ),
mistle-thrush; **L:** Kite.

EGG SHAPE

MOST BIRDS' EGGS, like the familiar hen's egg, are oval, that is to say, they are longer than broad, and blunter at one end than at the other. Those which do not conform to this general description are either elliptical, with both ends equally blunt, or near-spherical. In some eggs also the typical oval is sharply pointed at one end into the shape of a pear.

Elliptical: **S:** Barred woodpecker, wryneck, swift, STORM-PETREL; **MS:** Pied woodpecker, F/T PETREL; **M:** Nightjar, turtle-dove, hoopoe, merlin, sparrowhawk, hobby, green woodpecker, stock-dove, London pigeon, kestrel, barn-owl, l/e owl, *rock-dove*, DABCHICK, B/N GREBE, SLAVONIAN GREBE, TEAL; **ML:** Peregrine, stone-curlew, woodpigeon, Montagu's

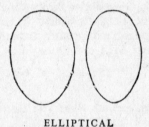

ELLIPTICAL

harrier, hen-harrier, com buzzard, *marsh-harrier*, GARGANEY, TUFTED DUCK, MANDARIN DUCK, WIGEON, COM POCHARD, G/C GREBE, COM SCOTER, GADWALL, SHOVELER; **L:** Kite, PINTAIL, MALLARD, EIDER, R/B MERGANSER, SHELD-DUCK, GOOSANDER; **VL:** Golden eagle, *greylag goose*, *bittern*, *heron*, SHAG, CORMORANT, GANNET; **H:** CANADA GOOSE, MUTE SWAN.

Pear-shaped: **S:** *L/r plover*, R/N PHALAROPE; **MS:** *Dunlin, ringed plover, com sandpiper*; **M:** Golden plover, lapwing,

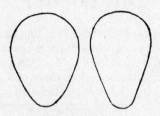

PEAR-SHAPED

com snipe, com redshank, greenshank; **ML:** *Whimbrel, bl/t godwit*, GUILLEMOT; **L:** *Curlew.*

Spherical (or nearly so): **S:** *Kingfisher*; **MS:** Lit owl; **ML:** S/e owl, tawny owl.

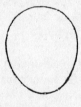

SPHERICAL

EGG COLOUR

THE COLOURING of eggs can be divided into the ground-colour, and the superimposed markings in the shape of spots, speckles, blotches, hair-marks and streaks. Many eggs have the ground-colour only, but the majority, especially of the song-birds are marked in some way. Occasionally the markings are so heavy, as for instance often with the kestrel, as completely to obscure the ground-colour. With other birds, such as the grebes, the basic ground-colour is normally obscured by staining in the nest after the egg has been laid.

In the following lists, each ground-colour is divided into 'marked' and 'unmarked' (the many rare unmarked varieties of normally marked eggs have been ignored). The marking of eggs is so variable in colour that it was felt that no useful purpose would be served by listing eggs according to the colour of their markings. The very few eggs with noticeable streaks (as distinct from hair-marks, or hair-like streaks) are, however, shown under a separate heading.

Blue—Marked: VS: Goldfinch (pale), siskin (pale), redpoll, *marsh-warbler* (pale); **S:** Linnet (pale), twite, spotted flycatcher (pale), greenfinch (pale), wheatear (occ), cirl-bunting (pale), snow-bunting (pale), crossbill (pale), hawfinch (pale); **MS:** Song-thrush; **M:** Cuckoo, jackdaw (pale); **ML:** Hen-harrier (pale, occ); **L:** GT BLACK-BACK.

Blue—Unmarked: VS: Pied flycatcher; **S:** Com redstart, wheatear, hedge-sparrow; **MS:** Starling; **ML:** Montagu's harrier (pale), hen-harrier (pale), *marsh-harrier* (pale), KITTI-WAKE (greyish).

Blue-Green—Marked: VS: Whinchat, stonechat; **S:** Robin, bullfinch, chaffinch; **MS:** *Dunlin*; **M:** Ring-ouzel, blackbird,

148

mistle-thrush, BLACK GUILLEMOT, B/H GULL; **ML:** Rook, carrion-crow, hooded crow, COM GULL, RAZORBILL, GUILLEMOT; **L:** Raven, LESSER BLACK-BACK, HERRING-GULL.

Blue-Green—Unmarked: VL: *Heron.*

Brown—Marked (see also Buff): **VS:** *Sedge-warbler* (yellowish), **S:** Tree-pipit, r/b shrike (pale), *reed-bunting* (olive); **MS:** Corn-bunting (pale), skylark, quail (marbled), *dunlin* (olive); **M:** Woodcock, B/H GULL; **ML:** *Whimbrel, Sandwich tern,* COM GULL (olive), KITTIWAKE, RAZORBILL, GUILLEMOT, ARCTIC SKUA; **L:** *Curlew,* LESSER BLACK-BACK, HERRING-GULL, R/T DIVER (olive), GT SKUA, B/T DIVER (olive), GT BLACK-BACK.

Brown—Unmarked (see also Buff); **S:** Nightingale (olive); **M:** Com partridge (pale olive), green woodpecker (stained), DABCHICK (stained), B/N GREBE (stained), SLAVONIAN GREBE (stained); **ML:** G/C GREBE (stained); **L:** Pheasant (pale olive); **VL:** *Bittern* (olive).

Buff or Stone-colour—Marked: **S:** Lesser whitethroat, com whitethroat, chaffinch, meadow-pipit, hawfinch, *reed-bunting, l/r plover, Kentish plover, yellow wagtail,* R/N PHALAROPE; **MS:** Dotterel, *grey wagtail, dunlin, ringed plover, com sandpiper, spotted crake*; **M:** Golden plover, lapwing, cuckoo, woodcock, ptarmigan, red grouse, r/l partridge, *lit tern, com snipe, water-rail, com redshank, greenshank, com tern, arctic tern, roseate tern,* MOORHEN, BLACK GUILLEMOT, B/H GULL; **ML:** Stone-curlew, black grouse, *whimbrel, bl/t godwit, Sandwich tern, avocet, oystercatcher,* COOT, COM GULL, KITTIWAKE, RAZORBILL, GUILLEMOT; **L:** Capercaillie, *curlew,* LESSER BLACK-BACK, HERRING-GULL, GT SKUA, GT BLACK-BACK.

Buff or Stone-colour—Unmarked: **M:** Com partridge, DABCHICK (stained), B/N GREBE (stained), SLAVONIAN GREBE (stained), TEAL; **ML:** GARGANEY, MANDARIN DUCK, WIGEON, G/C GREBE (stained), COM SCOTER, GADWALL, SHOVELER; **L:** Pheasant, R/B MERGANSER; **VL:** *Greylag goose,* SHAG (stained), CORMORANT (stained, GANNET (stained); **H;** CANADA GOOSE.

Green—Marked (see also Blue-Green): **VS:** Dartford warbler, *reed-warbler*, *marsh-warbler* (pale), *sedge-warbler*; **S:** Com whitethroat, garden-warbler, blackcap, spotted flycatcher (pale), cirl-bunting, snow-bunting, hawfinch (pale), r/b shrike (pale); **M:** Blackbird, cuckoo, jay, *com snipe* (olive), lapwing (olive); **ML:** Chough (pale), magpie, rook, *whimbrel*, *bl/t godwit*, ARCTIC SKUA; **L:** *Curlew*, R/T DIVER (olive), GT SKUA.

Green—Unmarked: **S:** Nightingale (olive); **ML:** TUFTED DUCK (greyish), COM POCHARD (greyish), SHOVELER; **L:** MALLARD, EIDER, R/B MERGANSER; **H:** MUTE SWAN (pale).

Grey—Marked: **S:** Tree-pipit, wood-lark (pale), hawfinch (pale), *rock-pipit*, *yellow wagtail* (occ); **MS:** Corn-bunting, skylark, pied wagtail (pale); **M:** Cuckoo, woodcock, *com tern*, *roseate tern*; **ML:** KITTIWAKE (bluish).

Grey—Unmarked: **M:** Hoopoe; **ML:** TUFTED DUCK (greenish), COM POCHARD (greenish); **H:** MUTE SWAN (pale).

Olive—Marked: **S:** *Reed-bunting*; **MS:** Dunlin; **M:** *Com snipe*; **ML:** COM GULL; **L:** R/T DIVER, B/T DIVER.

Olive—Unmarked: **S:** Nightingale; **M:** Com partridge (pale); **L:** Pheasant (pale); **VL:** Bittern.

Pink—Marked: **S:** R/b shrike (pale).

Purplish—Marked: **S:** Yellowhammer.

Reddish or Rufous—Marked: **S:** Tree-pipit, yellowhammer; **M:** Mistle-thrush.

Reddish or Rufous—Suffused: **M:** Merlin, hobby, kestrel, ptarmigan, red grouse, r/l partridge; **ML:** Peregrine.

Streaked: S: Cirl-bunting, yellowhammer, *reed-bunting*; MS: Corn-bunting; ML: RAZORBILL, GUILLEMOT.

White—Marked: VS: Goldcrest, wren, willow-warbler, chiff-chaff, coal-tit, crested tit, blue tit, marsh-tit, willow-tit, tree-creeper, wood-warbler, grasshopper-warbler, Dartford warbler; S: Lesser Whitethroat, garden-warbler, blackcap, robin, nuthatch, gt tit, l/t tit, tree-sparrow, house-sparrow, greenfinch, meadow-pipit, wood-lark (greyish), yellow-hammer, crossbill, r/b shrike (cream), *bearded tit*; MS: Pied wagtail (greyish), swallow, F/T PETREL; M: Golden oriole, nightjar (marbled), corncrake, sparrowhawk, *roseate tern* (cream), PUFFIN; ML: Chough, com buzzard, *Sandwich tern*, RAZORBILL, GUILLEMOT; L: Kite, GT SKUA (cream); VL: Golden eagle.

White—Unmarked: VS: House-martin, *sand-martin*; S: Black redstart, robin (occ), barred woodpecker, wryneck, swift, *kingfisher*, STORM-PETREL; MS: Lit owl, pied woodpecker, *dipper*; M: Turtledove, green woodpecker (liable to stain), stock-dove, London pigeon, eastern collard dove, barn-owl, l/e owl, *rock-dove*, MANX SHEARWATER, DABCHICK (liable to stain), PUFFIN, B/N GREBE (liable to stain), SLAVONIAN GREBE (ditto); ML: S/e owl, tawny owl, woodpigeon, Montagu's harrier, WIGEON (cream), FULMAR, G/C GREBE (liable to stain), COM SCOTER (cream); L: SHELD-DUCK (cream), GOOSANDER (cream); VL: *Greylag goose*, SHAG (liable to stain), COR-MORANT (ditto), GANNET (ditto); H: CANADA GOOSE, MUTE SWAN.

Yellowish—Marked: VS: Goldcrest, *sedge-warbler;* S: Snow-bunting, *yellow wagtail;* ML: GUILLEMOT, ARCTIC SKUA; L: R/T DIVER, GT SKUA.

Yellowish—Unmarked: M: Hoopoe, green woodpecker (stained); L: PINTAIL; VL: *Greylag goose.*

NESTLINGS

THIS SECTION of the key covers only the nestlings of the song-birds and some of their close allies, such as the woodpeckers.

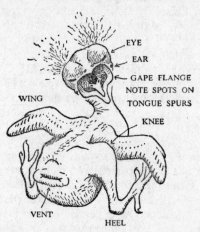

Many nestlings of other species can run about almost as soon as they are hatched, and so can rarely provide a clue to the identity of a nest.

Down Absent: VS: Dartford warbler, *reed-warbler, marsh-warbler, sedge-warbler*; **S:** Lesser whitethroat, com white-throat, garden-warbler, blackcap, tree-sparrow, house-sparrow, barred woodpecker, swift, r/b shrike, *bearded tit, kingfisher*; **MS:** Pied woodpecker; **M:** Green woodpecker, cuckoo, jay; **ML:** Magpie.

Mouth Orange or Orange-Yellow: VS: Goldcrest, willow-warbler, coal-tit, blue tit, pied flycatcher, whinchat, *reed-warbler, sedge-warbler*; **S:** Lesser whitethroat, spotted fly-catcher, com redstart, gt tit, chaffinch (palate), wheatear, hedge-sparrow, tree-pipit, nightingale, r/b shrike, *yellow wagtail*; MS: Pied wagtail, *grey wagtail, dipper*; M: Cuckoo.

Mouth Pink: S: Linnet, twite, com whitethroat (back), garden-warbler (reddish), blackcap, nuthatch (dark flesh), tree-sparrow, house-sparrow (yellowish), greenfinch, bull-finch, chaffinch (cerise), barred woodpecker (flesh), cirl-bunting, yellowhammer, crossbill (yellow and purplish-pink), hawfinch, wryneck (flesh), swift (flesh), *reed-bunting* (cerise), kingfisher (flesh); MS: Corn-bunting (flesh); M: Golden oriole, hoopoe, jackdaw (purplish), stock-dove, jay; ML: Chough, magpie (cerise), rook (cerise), carrion-crow (cerise), hooded crow (cerise); L: Raven (cerise).

Mouth Red: VS: Goldfinch, redpoll; S: Garden-warbler (pinkish), meadow-pipit (carmine), *rock-pipit, bearded tit.*

Mouth Yellow: VS: Wren, chiffchaff, crested tit, marsh-tit, willow-tit, tree-creeper, wood-warbler, grasshopper-warbler, Dartford warbler, stonechat, house-martin, *sand-martin, marsh-warbler*; S: Com whitethroat (front), black redstart, robin, l/t tit, house-sparrow (pinkish), wood-lark, crossbill (purplish-pink); MS: Skylark, swallow, starling, song-thrush; M: Ring-ouzel, blackbird, mistle-thrush.

Mouth-Spots: VS: Redpoll; S: Bullfinch, *bearded tit*; ML: Chough, magpie.

Tongue-Spots (Black): VS: Grasshopper-warbler, Dartford warbler, *reed-warbler, marsh-warbler, sedge-warbler*; S: Lesser whitethroat, com whitethroat, hedge-sparrow, wood-lark; MS: Skylark.

Tongue-Spots (Other Colours): VS: Willow-warbler (brown); S: Garden-warbler (purple), blackcap (brown), tree-sparrow (occ, dark), meadow-pipit (white), tree-pipit (yellow), haw-finch (white), swift (brown); ML: Magpie (white).

THE GREAT AUK

In Memoriam

18440 B.C. to A.D. 1844

APPENDIX I—NEST BOXES

By R. A. Richardson

IT IS ALWAYS a joy to have birds actually nesting in the garden, and what better way is there of encouraging them than by putting up a few nesting-boxes in sheltered positions? Armed with some suitable wood, a few nails, a saw and a hammer even the most unskilled 'handyman' can soon produce some workmanlike boxes which should give many seasons' service. The simpler and more Spartan the design, the better. Avoid like the plague the fancy châlet-type contraptions which go so well with plaster gnomes and cement frogs. The following notes and sketches are designed to assist in the planning, making and siting of some elementary boxes.

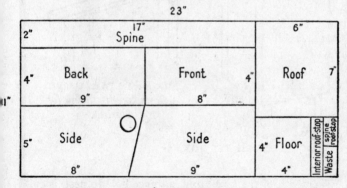

FIG. 1. TIT BOX

Tit Box

First obtain a piece of ½-in. thick deal boarding 23 in. × 11 in. and mark out and cut the sections as illustrated in Fig. 1, making allowance for the width of the saw-cuts.

Then assemble as in Fig. 2, when the lid, as shown in Fig. 3, can be fastened shut with a small brass hook.

Different species need entrance holes of different diameters and the following is a rough guide to the best sizes.

$1\frac{1}{8}$-in. Blue, Coal- and Marsh-Tits.

$1\frac{1}{4}$-in. Great Tit and Tree-Sparrow.

$1\frac{1}{2}$-in. Wryneck, Redstart, Pied Flycatcher, Nuthatch and House-Sparrow.

2-in.   Starling (other dimensions of box doubled).

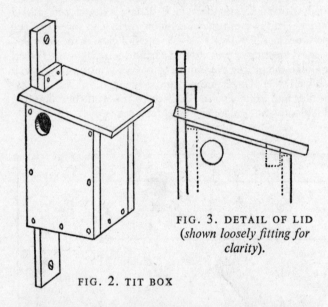

FIG. 3. DETAIL OF LID
(*shown loosely fitting for clarity*).

FIG. 2. TIT BOX

The depth of the box, from entrance-hole to nest, is calculated to discourage the stronger nestlings from crowding to the hole and preventing the parent birds from entering to feed the remainder of the brood.

Creosote the outside of the box and allow to dry for several days before screwing it *firmly*, about 6 feet from the ground, to a tree-bole or wall in a position permanently sheltered from the blazing sun or cold winds.

Robin Box

Robins, spotted flycatchers or pied wagtails will use an open-fronted box from which the incubating bird can watch events outside.

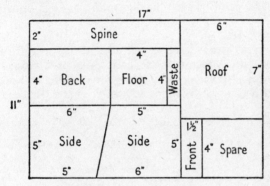

FIG. 4. ROBIN BOX

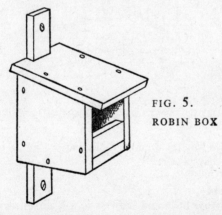

FIG. 5.

ROBIN BOX

The method of marking out and cutting the sections for this type of box is shown in Fig. 4, and Fig. 5 shows the finished box which should be sited not less than 4 feet from the ground (6 feet for flycatchers and wagtails) among ivy, wistaria, etc; on a wall or tree-trunk, again ensuring protection from direct sun, wind and cats. Flycatchers and wagtails will use these boxes in successive seasons, so once occupied reserve it for them. When more natural sites are scarce, blackbirds and song-thrushes will nest occasionally in a similar type of box but the dimensions must be doubled.

Swallow Ledge

In rural areas swallows will take readily to small ledges nailed up in the rafters of sheds, outhouses, barns, boat-houses and porches. Any odd piece of wood will do, provided it is about four or five inches square. Remember to

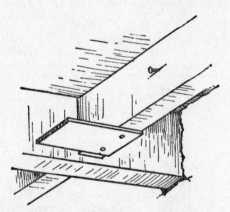

FIG. 6. SWALLOW'S LEDGE AMONG RAFTERS

leave a way for them to fly in and out of the building whenever they please.

Owl Tubs

Tawny, little and barn owls will sometimes take up residence in a strong apple tub fixed securely on its side in the main fork of a large tree.

158

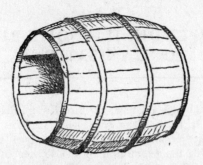

FIG. 7. OWL'S BOX MADE FROM APPLE TUB

General

Cats can be kept at bay by arranging gorse branches below the box. On no account should ammonia-soaked cotton-wool be left lying about for this purpose, as has been advocated. Birds are sure to pick it up for nest-material, with disastrous results.

The gnawing of marauding squirrels can be foiled by nailing a band of sheet metal round the entrance to the box. Mice can be a menace to eggs and young birds but one can do little about it.

Autumn is the best time of the year for siting the boxes. The birds then have plenty of time in which to accustom themselves to popping in and out for winter roosting.

When birds are in occupation the box should *never* be inspected more than once a day. It is a great mistake to place food against a nesting-box. The birds will find it soon enough without the resented interference from other birds flocking to feed there.

Full details of nest-boxes for these and many other kinds of birds will be found in the British Trust for Ornithology's Field Guide 'Nest-Boxes', by Edwin Cohen and Bruce Campbell, obtainable for half a crown from the Trust at 2 King Edward Street, Oxford.

APPENDIX II — SOME BIRD ORGANISATIONS

British Ornithologists' Union, c/o Bird Room, British Museum (Natural History), Cromwell Road, London S.W.7. The premier bird organisation in the British Isles, which is concerned with the promotion of the science of ornithology throughout the world. Journal: *The Ibis* (quarterly).

British Trust for Ornithology, 2 King Edward St., Oxford. The society especially concerned with field ornithological research in the British Isles. Journal: *Bird Study* (quarterly).

Royal Society for the Protection of Birds, 25 Eccleston Square, London, S.W.1. The most important society concerned with the protection of birds and the conservation of their habitats in Great Britain. The society's educational work is largely carried out through the Junior Bird Recorders Club, open to young people aged 11–18. Journals: *Bird Notes* (quarterly); *J.B.R.C. Bulletin* (quarterly).

Wildfowl Trust, New Grounds, Slimbridge, Glos. The society especially concerned with the study, protection and conservation of wildfowl, ducks, geese and swans, throughout the world. Journal: Annual Report.

A list of local natural history societies and bird clubs in the British Isles will be found in the *Directory of Natural History Societies,* published by the British Association (18 Adam St., London, W.C.2.) for 21s. 6d. post free.

Details of the 14 bird observatories now operating in the British Isles may be had from the British Trust for Ornithology. They are: Fair Isle (Shetland), Isle of May (Fife), Spurn Point

(Yorks), Gibraltar Point (Lincs), Cley (Norfolk), Dungeness (Kent), Jersey (Channel Islands), Portland (Dorset), Lundy (N. Devon), New Grounds (Glos.), Skokholm (Pembs.), Bardsey (N Wales), Copeland (N Ireland), Saltee (Co Wexford).

APPENDIX III

SYSTEMATIC LIST OF BIRDS IN THE TEXT

FOR THE BENEFIT of those who are interested in such things, the following list gives all the birds mentioned in the text in the new Wetmore systematic order, recently adopted as standard in Britain. It has long been current in America and elsewhere in the world. The object of this arrangement is to present the various families of birds in approximately the order in which they appeared in the evolutionary time-scale. It therefore begins with the most primitive families, the grebes and divers, which even now have a faintly reptilian look, and ends with the various families of song-birds, known as passerines, which are the most advanced in the evolutionary scale.

DIVER FAMILY

Black-throated diver	*Colymbus arcticus*
Great northern diver	*C. immer*
Red-throated diver	*C. stellatus*

GREBE FAMILY

Great crested grebe	*Podiceps cristatus*
Slavonian grebe	*P. auritus*
Black-necked grebe	*P. caspicus*
Dabchick	*P. ruficollis*

SHEARWATER FAMILY

Fork-tailed petrel	*Oceanodroma leucorrhoa*
Storm-petrel	*Hydrobates pelagicus*
Manx shearwater	*Procellaria puffinus*
Fulmar	*Fulmarus glacialis*

BOOBY FAMILY

Gannet	*Sula bassana*

CORMORANT FAMILY

Cormorant	*Phalacrocorax carbo*
Shag	*P. aristotelis*

THE POCKET GUIDE TO NESTS AND EGGS

HERON FAMILY
Heron	*Ardea cinerea*
Little bittern	*Ixobrychus minutus*
Bittern	*Botaurus stellaris*

STORK FAMILY
White stork	*Ciconia ciconia*

SPOONBILL FAMILY
Spoonbill	*Platalea leucorodia*

DUCK FAMILY
Mallard	*Anas platyrhynchos*
Teal	*A. crecca*
Garganey	*A. querquedula*
Gadwall	*A. strepera*
Wigeon	*A. penelope*
Pintail	*A. acuta*
Shoveler	*Spatula clypeata*
Red-crested pochard	*Netta rufina*
Scaup	*Aythya marila*
Tufted duck	*A. fuligula*
Common pochard	*A. ferina*
Goldeneye	*Bucephala clangula*
Long-tailed duck	*Clangula hyemalis*
Velvet scoter	*Melanitta fusca*
Surf-scoter	*M. perspicillata*
Common scoter	*M. nigra*
Eider	*Somateria mollissima*
King-eider	*S. spectabilis*
Red-breasted merganser	*Mergus serrator*
Goosander	*M. merganser*
Smew	*M. albellus*
Mandarin duck	*Aix galericulata*

Sheld-duck	*Tadorna tadorna*
Grey lag-goose	*Anser anser*
Canada goose	*Branta canadensis*
Mute swan	*Cygnus olor*
Whooper swan	*C. cygnus*

FALCON FAMILY
Golden eagle	*Aquila chrysaëtos*
Common buzzard	*Buteo buteo*
Sparrowhawk	*Accipiter nisus*
Goshawk	*A. gentilis*
Kite	*Milvus milvus*
Sea-eagle	*Haliæëtus albicilla*
Honey-buzzard	*Pernis apivorus*
Marsh-harrier	*Circus aeruginosus*
Hen-harrier	*C. cyaneus*
Montagu's harrier	*C. pygargus*
Osprey	*Pandion haliaetus*
Hobby	*Falco subbuteo*
Peregrine	*F. peregrinus*
Merlin	*F. columbarius*
Kestrel	*F. tinnunculus*

GROUSE FAMILY
Red grouse	*Lagopus scoticus*
Ptarmigan	*L. mutus*
Black grouse	*Lyrurus tetrix*
Capercaillie	*Tetrao urogallus*

PHEASANT FAMILY
Red-legged partridge	*Alectoris rufa*
Common partridge	*Perdix perdix*
Quail	*Coturnix coturnix*
Pheasant	*Phasanius colchicus*

162

APPENDIX

CRANE FAMILY
Common crane   *Megalornis grus*

RAIL FAMILY
Water-rail	*Rallus aquaticus*
Spotted crake	*Porzana porzana*
Baillon's crake	*P. pusilla*
Little crake	*P. parva*
Corncrake	*Crex crex*
Moorhen	*Gallinula chloropus*
Coot	*Fulica atra*

BUSTARD FAMILY
Great bustard   *Otis tarda*

OYSTERCATCHER FAMILY
Oystercatcher   *Haematopus ostralegus*

PLOVER FAMILY
Lapwing	*Vanellus vanellus*
Ringed plover	*Charadrius hiaticula*
Little ringed plover	*C. dubius*
Kentish plover	*C. alexandrinus*
Golden plover	*C. apricarius*
Dotterel	*C. morinellus*
Turnstone	*Arenaria interpres*

SANDPIPER FAMILY
Common snipe	*Capella gallinago*
Jack snipe	*Lymnocryptes minimus*
Woodcock	*Scolopax rusticola*
Curlew	*Numenius arquata*
Whimbrel	*N. phaeopus*
Black-tailed godwit	*Limosa limosa*
Bar-tailed godwit	*L. lapponica*
Green sandpiper	*Tringa ochropus*
Wood-sandpiper	*T. glareola*
Common sandpiper	*T. hypoleucos*
Redshank	*T. totanus*
Greenshank	*T. nebularia*
Purple sandpiper	*Calidris maritima*
Temminck's stint	*C. temminckii*
Dunlin	*C. alpina*
Ruff	*Philomachus pugnax*

AVOCET FAMILY
Avocet	*Recurvirostra avosetta*
Stilt	*Himantopus himantopus*

PHALAROPE FAMILY
Red-necked phalarope   *Phalaropus lobatus*

STONE-CURLEW FAMILY
Stone-curlew   *Burhinus oedicnemus*

SKUA FAMILY
Arctic skua	*Stercorarius parasiticus*
Great skua	*S. skua*

GULL FAMILY
Great black-back	*Larus marinus*
Lesser black-back	*L. fuscus*
Herring-gull	*L. argentatus*
Common gull	*L. canus*
Black-headed gull	*L. ridibundus*
Kittiwake	*Rissa tridactyla*
Black tern	*Chlidonias niger*
Gull-billed tern	*Gelochelidon nilotica*

Common tern	*Sterna hirundo*
Arctic tern	*S. macrura*
Roseate tern	*S. dougallii*
Little tern	*S. albifrons*
Sandwich tern	*S. sandvicensis*

AUK FAMILY
Razorbill	*Alca torda*
Great auk	*Alca impennis*
Little auk	*Plautus alle*
Guillemot	*Uria aalge*
Black guillemot	*U. grylle*
Puffin	*Fratercula arctica*

SAND-GROUSE FAMILY
Pallas's sand-grouse	*Syrrhaptes paradoxus*

DOVE FAMILY
Stock-dove	*Columbia oenas*
Rock-dove and London pigeon	*C. livia*
Woodpigeon	*C. palumbus*
Turtle-dove	*Streptopelia turtur*
Eastern collared dove	*S. decaocto*

CUCKOO FAMILY
Cuckoo	*Cuculus canorus*

OWL FAMILY
Barn-owl	*Tyto alba*
Little owl	*Athene noctua*
Tawny owl	*Strix aluco*
Long-eared owl	*Asio otus*
Short-eared owl	*A. flammeus*

NIGHTJAR FAMILY
Nightjar	*Caprimulgus europaeus*

SWIFT FAMILY
Swift	*Apus apus*

KINGFISHER FAMILY
Kingfisher	*Alcedo atthis*

BEE-EATER FAMILY
Bee-eater	*Merops apiaster*

HOOPOE FAMILY
Hoopoe	*Upopa epops*

WOODPECKER FAMILY
Green woodpecker	*Picus viridis*
Pied woodpecker	*Dendrocopos major*
Barred woodpecker	*D. minor*
Great black woodpecker	*Dryocopus martius*
Wryneck	*Jynx torquilla*

LARK FAMILY
Wood-lark	*Lullula arborea*
Skylark	*Alauda arvensis*

SWALLOW FAMILY
Swallow	*Hirundo rustica*
House-martin	*Delichon urbica*
Sand-martin	*Riparia riparia*

ORIOLE FAMILY
Golden oriole	*Oriolus oriolus*

CROW FAMILY
Raven	*Corvus corax*
Carrion-crow	*C. corone*
Hooded crow	*C. cornix*
Rook	*C. frugilegus*
Jackdaw	*C. monedula*
Magpie	*Pica pica*
Jay	*Garrulus glandarius*
Chough	*Coracia pyrrhocorax*

APPENDIX

TIT FAMILY

Great tit	*Parus major*
Blue tit	*P. caeruleus*
Coal tit	*P. ater*
Crested tit	*P. cristatus*
Marsh-tit	*P. palustris*
Willow-tit	*P. atricapillus*
Long-tailed tit	*Aegithalos caudatus*
Bearded tit	*Panurus biarmicus*

NUTHATCH FAMILY

Nuthatch	*Sitta europaea*

CREEPER FAMILY

Tree-creeper	*Certhia familiaris*

WREN FAMILY

Wren	*Troglodytes troglodytes*

DIPPER FAMILY

Dipper	*Cinclus cinclus*

THRUSH FAMILY

Mistle-thrush	*Turdus viscivorus*
Fieldfare	*T. pilaris*
Song-thrush	*T. ericetorum*
Redwing	*T. musicus*
Ring-ouzel	*T. torquatus*
Blackbird	*T. merula*
Wheatear	*Oenanthe oenanthe*
Stonechat	*Saxicola torquata*
Whinchat	*S. rubetra*
Common redstart	*Phoenicurus phoenicurus*
Black redstart	*P. ochruros*
Nightingale	*Luscinia megarhynchos*
Robin	*Erithacus rubecula*

WARBLER FAMILY

Grasshopper-warbler	*Locustella naevia*
Moustached warbler	*Lusciniola melanopogon*
Reed-warbler	*Acrocephalus scirpaceus*
Marsh-warbler	*A. palustris*
Sedge-warbler	*A. schoenobaenus*
Melodious warbler	*Hippolais polyglotta*
Icterine warbler	*H. icterina*
Blackcap	*Sylvia atricapilla*
Garden-warbler	*S. borin*
Common whitethroat	*S. communis*
Lesser whitethroat	*S. curruca*
Dartford warbler	*S. undata*
Willow-warbler	*Phylloscopus trochilus*
Chiffchaff	*P. collybita*
Wood-warbler	*P. sibilatrix*

KINGLET FAMILY

Goldcrest	*Regulus regulus*
Firecrest	*R. ignicapillus*

FLYCATCHER FAMILY

Spotted flycatcher	*Muscicapa striata*
Pied flycatcher	*M. hypoleuca*

ACCENTOR FAMILY

Hedge-sparrow	*Prunella modularis*

WAGTAIL FAMILY

Meadow-pipit	*Anthus pratensis*
Tree-pipit	*A. trivialis*
Rock-pipit	*A. spinoletta*
Pied and white wagtails	*Motacilla alba*
Grey wagtail	*M. cinerea*
Yellow wagtail	*M. flava*

165

SHRIKE FAMILY

| Woodchat | *Lanius senator* |
| Red-backed shrike | *L. collurio* |

STARLING FAMILY

| Starling | *Sturnus vulgaris* |

FINCH FAMILY

Hawfinch	*Coccothraustes coccothraustes*
Greenfinch	*Chloris chloris*
Goldfinch	*Carduelis carduelis*
Siskin	*C. spinus*
Linnet	*C. cannabina*
Twite	*C. flavirostris*
Lesser redpoll	*C. flammea*

Serin	*Serinus canarius*
Bullfinch	*Pyrrhula pyrrhula*
Crossbill	*Loxia curvirostra*
Chaffinch	*Fringilla coelebs*
Brambling	*F. montifringilla*
Yellow-hammer	*Emberiza citrinella*
Corn-bunting	*E. calandra*
Cirl-bunting	*E. cirlus*
Reed-bunting	*E. schoeniclus*
Snow-bunting	*Plectrophenax nivalis*

SPARROW FAMILY

| House-sparrow | *Passer domesticus* |
| Tree-sparrow | *P. montanus* |

There was an old man with a beard
Who said, 'It is just as I feared,
Four larks and a wren,
Two owls and a hen
Have all built their nests in my beard'.

EDWARD LEAR

166

INDEX

Figures in heavy type refer to plates

The companion
guide you also need

COLLINS POCKET GUIDE TO BRITISH BIRDS

TEXT BY R. S. R. FITTER
ILLUSTRATED BY R. A. RICHARDSON

"The most complete book on bird-watching I have yet come across. Simplifies identification enormously."

JOHN MARSHALL IN THE EVENING NEWS

"It is difficult to believe that any information useful to the bird-watcher or ornithologist in the matter of identification has been omitted. This is a remarkable production."

THE FIELD

"Undeniably a good 'guide'. I know of no book so well and completely illustrated at the price." THE NATURALIST

"... A remarkable book—remarkable because here for the first time we have an identification book which presupposes no knowledge of bird classification but enables the observer to name a bird by its obvious characteristics of colour, size, shape, flight and habit." S. P. B. MAIS IN THE OXFORD MAIL

64 pages of colour plates, 1,000 illustrations in all

In the same series

COLLINS POCKET GUIDE TO WILD FLOWERS

BY R. S. R. FITTER
AND DAVID McCLINTOCK

"Excellent. I doubt if any country has a popular guide to its plants so inclusive, so intelligently arranged, and so generously illustrated. Here you have the likenesses of more than 1,300 plants, nearly all of them drawn from living specimens, in one flowering season, by a team of seven draughtsmen; 600 are in colour, leaving black and white for plants with green and white flowers, grasses, sedges, horsetails, ferns, etc. A feat of publishing which should be standard in its class for half a century."

GEOFFREY GRIGSON IN THE OBSERVER

"Compiled with skill and precision, it is arranged and signposted so as to make things as easy as possible for the botanical innocent abroad in Britain."
SUNDAY TIMES

"The miracle of miracles is that almost as many species are illustrated as included. The colour plates show an abundance and a generosity no one could have hoped for. It is a lesson to lazy publishers, and it should at last clear much feeble rubbish out of shops and shelves."
LISTENER

64 pages of colour plates

In the same series

COLLINS POCKET GUIDE TO THE SEA SHORE

BY JOHN BARRETT
AND C. M. YONGE

"Here is your book if you want a holiday along the coast to be more than a blind laziness . . . so excellent a book."

"Written by the two greatest authorities on marine biology in the British Isles, sets out to enable *anyone* to identify the animals and plants to be found on the sea shore . . . a pretty ambitious objective; all I can say is that the authors have achieved it triumphantly. They have succeeded in packing into the 255-odd pages a simply fantastic amount of information about each species. They have done this in simple and sometimes vivid language with the use of a minimum of technical terms. It is rare indeed to find specialists writing so clearly for the non-specialist public. Some of the best colour plates I have ever seen. A book which it would be difficult to praise too highly."   BRIAN VESEY-FITZGERALD, BIRMINGHAM POST

"John Barrett and Professor C. M. Yonge, one of the best-known marine biologists in the world, together with a brilliant team of artists, have compiled a magnificent pocket guide which is indeed a Baedecker of the Sea Shore."

LEO WALMSLEY, YORKSHIRE POST

40 pages of colour plates

N

45
MILES TO
SCILLY IS.

0   25   50
MILES